BEYOND THE BASICS

gourd art

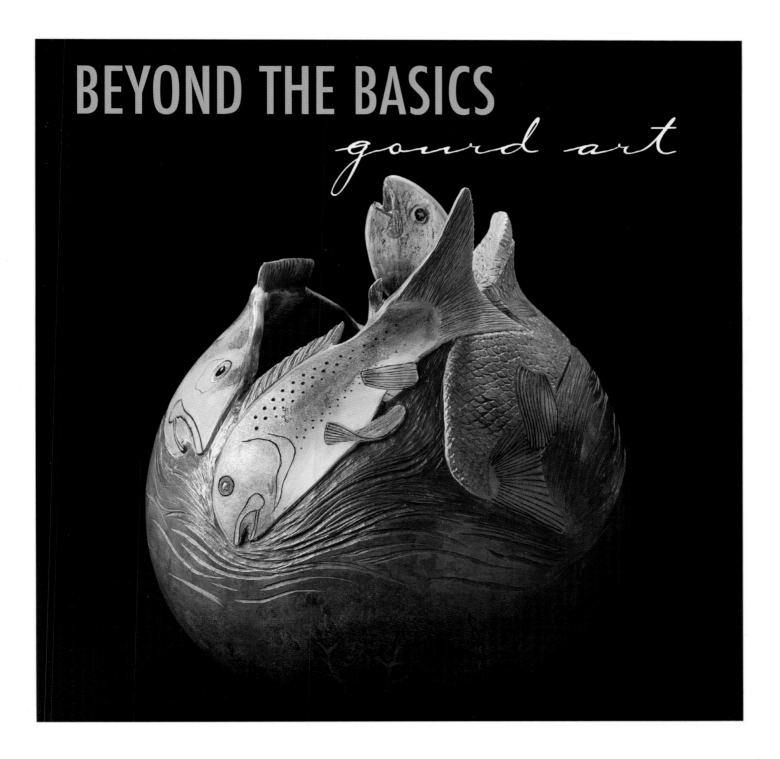

BEYOND THE BASICS

gourd art

DAVID MACFARLANE

Sterling Publishing Co., Inc. New York

A Sterling/Chapelle Book

Chapelle, Ltd.
  P.O. Box 9252, Ogden, UT 84409
  (801) 621-2777 • (801) 621-2788 Fax
  e-mail: chapelle@chapelleltd.com
  Web site: www.chapelleltd.com

Every effort has been made to ensure that all information in this book is
accurate. However, due to differing conditions, tools, and individual skills,
the publisher cannot be responsible for any injuries, losses, and/or other
damages which may result from the use of the information in this book.

This volume is meant to stimulate craft ideas. If readers are unfamiliar or
not proficient in a skill necessary to attempt a project, we urge that
they refer to an instructional book specifically addressing the required
technique.

Library of Congress Cataloging-in-Publication Data

Macfarlane, David, 1965-
  Beyond the basics : gourd art / David Macfarlane.
     p. cm.
  Includes bibliographical references and index.
  ISBN 1-4027-1060-7 (alk. paper)
  1. Gourd craft I. Title.

TT873.5.M33 2005
745.5--dc22
                                            2005018756

10 9 8 7 6 5 4 3 2
Published by Sterling Publishing Co., Inc.
387 Park Avenue South, New York, NY 10016
©2006 by David Macfarlane
Distributed in Canada by Sterling Publishing
c/o Canadian Manda Group, 165 Dufferin Street
Toronto, Ontario, Canada M6K 3H6
Distributed in Great Britain by Chrysalis Books Group PLC,
The Chrysalis Building, Bramley Road, London W10 6SP, England
Distributed in Australia by Capricorn Link (Australia) Pty. Ltd.
P.O. Box 704, Windsor, NSW 2756, Australia
Printed and Bound in China
All Rights Reserved

Sterling ISBN 1-4027-1060-7

For information about custom editions, special sales, premium and
corporate purchases, please contact Sterling Special Sales Department at
800-805-5489 or specialsales@sterlingpub.com

Table of Contents

Foreword

"DID YOU KNOW THAT PEOPLE MAKE VESSELS FROM GOURDS?"

This question was my introduction to gourds in the summer of 2000. I was invited to make a bowl at a friend's house and, unfortunately, cracked the gourd I was working on. Too embarrassed to ask for another, I chose instead to ask for a saw, cut the gourd in half, and made my first gourd mask. Who could have known that my friend's question would lead me into a whole new world and career?

Vessels are only the tip of the iceberg in the world of gourds. Yes, there are artists making the most unbelievable vessels, and that's just the beginning. There are artists who make sculptures, masks, functional creations, and free-form mixed-media pieces; creative artisans are using gourds, clay, and found objects to create beauty that no usual canvas can produce. The only boundaries are within one's own imagination.

My approach to gourds is similar to everything I've ever tried: jump right in and see what happens. I didn't take any of the amazing classes that are offered now and every technique I've tried has had a learning curve that sent me to places I never would have thought to try. It's the mistakes that have been my greatest gift. Each mask I've set out to create has begun with a finished face in my mind's eye, yet I've never had one turn out the way I thought it would. A simple mistake often changed the mask's personality and sent me in new directions. On my next mask, I made that same "mistake," but this time intentionally! What a wonderful thing.

It may seem odd to hear me talk about personalities and features on gourds, but it's true. These masks become a presence and develop their essence in addition to, not as a result of, what I do. I feel humbled to look at the finished product, to see a face on the wall that evokes an emotion or an expression. There are times these faces are beyond what I feel capable of, and the awe of seeing more than I crafted is the reason I continue as an artist. I am honored to write the foreword to this book and to see the amazing talent that's represented here. I am very familiar with some of the artists and their skills and am thrilled to be introduced to the others.

In the upcoming chapters, you'll find techniques that are new and you'll see examples of artwork that will leave you amazed. These are the end result of an individual artist's vision, and sometimes the result of an artist's mistakes. Keep this in mind as you read their explanations and directions. Just as these artists have found their respective voices in gourd art, use these tools to find your own. As I said before, the only boundaries you will face are the limits of your own imagination.

Dave Sisk

A Gourd Story

by Jan Mohr Meng

Gourds can break your heart. In the year it takes to go from seed to canvas, a gourd is subject to many tragedies: too much water, too little water, bugs, fickle fate. If you plan your art on the vine, you will likely be frustrated. Through the summer, gourds will grow and flourish, or shrivel and succumb. The one you have your eye on will hang on almost to maturity, and then puny up and die.

Nonetheless, the fruit that makes it can be glorious: one of a kind and beautifully quirky; oddly shaped with unusual shell patterns; good sitters with flawless shells and fabulous stems. There's a gourd for every artisan and an artisan for every gourd.

An intact gourd is a beautiful natural objet d'art, but gourds can certainly be more than ornamental. Gourds have long been used by humankind in both art and utility. Ancient pottery shards bear a striking resemblance to gourd crockery that preceded the development of pottery. Perhaps no other plant has served humankind so well or so diversely. In addition to household use, gourds were also used as weaponry. Gourds were used to hold body parts in human sacrifice ceremonies. Fishing cultures use them to float nets. Gourds are featured in creation myths and folklore the world over.

When gourds are fresh on the vine, they are green and heavy, with moisture-saturated shells and pulp. As they mature, the moisture dissipates and they turn lighter green, pale green, yellowish. In the fall, they begin to look brown; and in winter, the skin that was once green is now black, moldy and fuzzy. It's the *Ugly Duckling* story in reverse; the beautiful becomes homely.

However, the ugliness is only on the outside, or maybe not even there; as in everything gourd, there are exceptions. Sometimes the epidermis dries in beautiful patterns that only the obtuse would decide to scrub off.

TOOLS

As a general rule, any tool that comes in handy in working with wood will work on gourds: sandpaper, drills and bits, saws, power tools. Of course, a number of tools are available specifically for gourds, and experienced gourd artists will certainly be familiar with those choices.

Necessity creates all sorts of inimitable tools. A bent piece of rebar can poke through small openings and work as a prod to break up pulp. A flattened piece of cast-off aluminum tubing can be an ideal scraper. Iced tea spoons work well in tight spaces. For most readers of this book, gourd-art tools will already be familiar. For others, it might be necessary to separate the respective tools into categories.

EXTERNAL CLEANING TOOLS: copper scrubbing pads, kitchen knives, dishwashing detergent, bleach

The use of bleach is intended to retard mold. However, a clean, thoroughly dry gourd will not mold, and a bleached, thoroughly-dry-on-the-outside-but-still-damp-inside gourd will, so whether or not to use it is the artist's discretion. With warm water and enthusiasm, the other tools should be all you need to get a gourd clean.

CUTTING/DRILLING TOOLS: mini jigsaw, rotary tool, power drill

When creating gourds with lids, or bowls with even edges, use a jigsaw. When creating gourds with irregular edges or carvings, use a power tool like a routing tool.

Cautionary Note: Always wear a dust mask or respirator when carving, cutting or sanding gourds. Protective eyewear is recommended. Make sure you have a good comfortable hold on the gourd, especially when using power tools and sharp tools.

INTERNAL CLEANING/SCRAPING TOOLS: old spoons, wire brushes, improvised scrapers, sandpaper

Generally, an old metal spoon should work well to scrape the pulp and seeds out of the interior of an open gourd. Gourd retailers do sell tools, however, specially made for cleaning the interior of gourds. When the pulp and seeds are removed, coarse sandpaper should be used to clean up the interior. Also helpful might be a round wire brush on a power drill or various sanding attachments available for rotary tools.

ADDITIONAL SUPPLIES: As can be seen within the chapters of this book, the supplies available to gourd artisans are limited only by imagination. Paints, dyes, inks, glues, waxes, and sealers—not to mention whole bunches of unorthodox items—fill the materials and tools lists that follow. The best approach will be to peruse the pages and determine what project is the most appealing. Go to the craft or gourd store then with a full knowledge of exactly what to buy.

CLEANING IT OFF

Some gourd-cleaning techniques involve scraping the skin off a green gourd, or perhaps cutting open a green gourd and filling the interior with water to hasten internal rot. Generally, gourds are cleaned after drying outside during the winter. In this way, nature takes its course. By February or March, the strong gourds have survived, the weaker ones are compost.

1. Gourd art begins with a conscientious cleaning of the outside shell. The absolute best way to clean the outside of the gourd is to make sure the gourd is wet—thoroughly, absolutely wet. Watch the weather, and make sure your gourds are out in the rain. Turn on the sprinkler and soak both the lawn and the gourds. Place them in a burlap bag or pillowcase and weight them down with stones or bricks in a full bathtub. You'll know they're sufficiently wet when you can easily scrape the epidermis off with a fingernail.

2. Get a bucket of water and a knitted copper or aluminum pot scrubber, the kind available at any grocery store (see photo 1). Add a bit of basic dishwashing detergent and scrub like there is no tomorrow. Cleaning gourds is messy business, so make sure you're outside or somewhere you can scrub with abandon. Pay careful attention to the areas around the stem and navel. A sharp kitchen knife used judiciously in these areas can remove stubborn soil and matter from indentations. Don't gouge. Just scrape gently. Rinse the gourd well and let it dry completely (see photo 2).

Note: Again, some people add a bit of bleach to the rinse water, but in my experience, this doesn't do much to retard mold. If a gourd is completely dry inside and out, it won't mold. If it's damp, some mold may appear, but this is usually superficial. Just wipe or scrub it off when you're ready to work with the gourd. A well-cleaned gourd takes paint, finishes, and dye more uniformly and inhibits mold and bacterial growth.

CUTTING IT OPEN

How you open a gourd is determined by what you wish to do with it. If the gourd is to be a bowl or will have a lid, the best tool to use is a small jigsaw.

1. First insert a utility knife—blade horizontal—into the gourd (see photo 3). Be very careful. Gourd shells are hard and the blade can slip. From this point, wear a dust mask. Gourd dust can be very irritating and potentially harmful when breathed into the lungs. Always wear a mask or respirator when cutting or carving gourds and when cleaning gourd interiors. Protective eyewear is also recommended.

2. Carefully insert jigsaw blade into the slit made by the utility knife (see photo 4). Make sure the jigsaw blade goes in as far as possible. Grip the gourd and turn on the jigsaw; hold the saw firmly against the gourd and saw completely around the gourd. If keeping the gourd top as a lid, remember to carve a key: a slight detour or jog in the line or pattern that will identify exactly where the lid and gourd line up.

3. For carving around a design to make an open vessel with an irregular rim, the best option is a rotary tool (see photo 5). Bits and blades are available for practically every need. When following patterns, high-speed cutters are most useful. With rotary tools, there is no need to make an opening slit with the utility knife. Simply hold the gourd firmly and comfortably, turn on the tool and follow the design that has been sketched or burned into the gourd shell. Don't rush the tool; feel its pace.

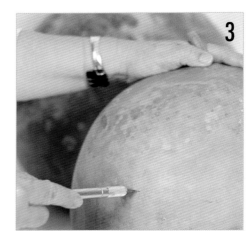

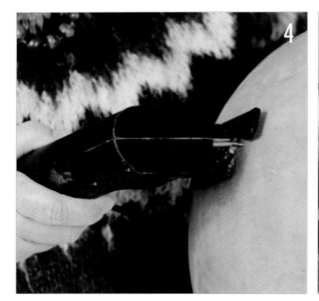

INTERNAL CLEANING

Opening a gourd is like opening a present: you never know for sure what you're going to see—or smell. Through the mystery of plant and soil chemistry, gourds can be bluish or pinkish inside. These colors are rare and memorable. Pulp and seeds can be bound together in a hard round mass, or seeds may lay loose on the bottom of the gourd. The gourd can be earthly fragrant and nutty, or eye-wateringly pungent.

An aromatically unpleasant gourd may be a lost cause. Some remedies include filling the offending gourd with ground coffee and water, or bleach and water, and soaking for some days. The coffee will stain the interior of the gourd. As with most home remedies, these are successful sometimes and most times not.

1. Using a metal spoon or gourd scraper, scrape the bulk of the seeds and pulp out of the gourd.

2. Using a minimum 150-grit sandpaper (see photo 6), sand the interior of the gourd smooth (a coarser grit may be more efficient). Shake the dust out from time to time. If the gourd has a lid, take great care not to sand the edges of the lid, which will alter the fit. When the sanding is done, take a blow dryer and blow out the remaining gourd dust.

3. In most cases, the scraper and sandpaper will be sufficient, with one distressing exception: the interior of the gourd is coated with a creamy white satin-looking lining. This sounds like it should be beautiful, and if it were uniform it would be. However, this is rarely the case, and trying to remove it takes great effort. Experience has shown that soaking this film with water, then working in small sections to pry it off is the best approach. It's slow and tedious, and it will test gourding mettle, but it can be done.

A gourd canvas doesn't just happen. It takes care and effort inside and out, but once done, the gourd will serve the artisan well and long (see photo 7).

6

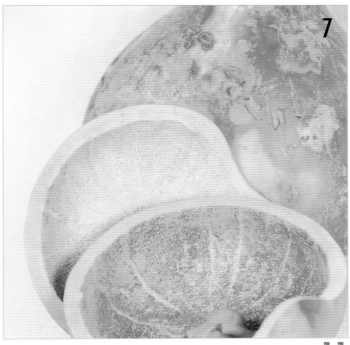

7

Artist

Jennifer Avery

Somewhere in the corner of Jennifer Avery's studio, the brushes and oils are crying out for attention. It seems that since their owner and former benefactor discovered gourd pyrography in 1999, they just don't get the favor they once enjoyed. Pity the poor brushes and oils once used for murals, but envy the gourds their justifiable attention. "Since crafting my first gourd," she recalls, "it's been a love affair. I found my true calling."

An art school graduate with a degree in illustration, Avery explains that the primary source of the gourd's appeal is that it plays countless roles. "It can be ornamented and enhanced in so many ways," she says. "I don't see an end to the possibilities."

Although she adorns gourds with "natural found materials" and recently started carving them as well, Avery's primary means of enhancement is pyrography, a technique she initially learned from her grandmother. "It wasn't until I dabbled with a gourd that I thought to use one of her old wood burners," she recalls. "Then the memories of her working and letting me play around with her burner came back."

For inspiration, Avery looks to the natural world and commonly depicts nature scenes or animals in intricately and delicately burned designs. Augmenting these scenes are the symmetrical swoops and arches of another interest, "medieval and renaissance illuminated manuscripts." Avery frequently uses Celtic knots and the like to create familiar, appealing, and effective border designs.

When she isn't working on them, Avery remains connected to gourds by sharing her enthusiasm with others. She is the founder of the Pennsylvania Gourd Society—the Chi Chapter of the American Gourd Society—and is active near her Lancaster County home, encouraging others to take up the craft. "People of all ages and levels of talent can make something to be proud of from a gourd," she says. "They can surprise themselves."

PEACE ON EARTH

BIRCH FOREST

CELTIC BESTIARY MOURNING DOVE

CELTIC KNOT BIRDHOUSE

In this functional work of art, the entrance to a birdhouse is decorated with a Celtic knot, providing both a home for wild creatures and a visual eye-catcher in the backyard. If your interest is primarily in the art, however, Avery recommends making the birdhouse a decorative piece only. "Pyrography fades rapidly when left out in the sun and weather, so the following directions will be for a decorative piece and not an actual residence for the birds."

MATERIALS
- Acrylic craft paint: Black
- Gourd
- Leather dye or wood stain: mahogany
- Spray urethane

TOOLS
- Compass
- Drill or utility knife
- Flexible ruler
- Kneadable eraser
- Masking tape (optional)
- Mini jigsaw
- Paintbrush with long handle
- Pencil
- Plastic grocery bag (optional)
- Sandpaper: fine grit
- Screwdriver: long for cleaning out gourd
- Wood-burning tool with all-purpose (standard) and shading tips

14

STEP ONE: Clean the outside of the gourd (see page 9). For this project, Avery chooses a pear-shaped gourd roughly 11" tall and 5½" around at its widest point.

STEP TWO: Map out the design area where the hole will be cut and the knot will be burned. Using a compass, position the fixed arm with the sharp end on the gourd where a circle slightly more than 4" in diameter will fit comfortably and be visible. Draw a circle 1½" in diameter (see photo 1). Expand the moveable compass arm ¼" and draw another circle. Draw two more circles, each ½" larger than the last, then expand the compass another ¼" and draw a final circle. At this point, a symmetrical bulls-eye design will be visible on the gourd surface.

STEP THREE: Draw the Celtic design on the gourd. Avery explains that "the two ¼" lines are border lines; the two ½" lines are design lines. Focus on the first ½" line drawn, which is the center of the design." In this piece, start by eyeballing four points equidistant apart at the top, bottom, right, and left on the center of the design. Mark three dots, roughly ½" apart, between each of the initial four dots (see photos 1 and 2). A flexible ruler is helpful in getting the dots located correctly.

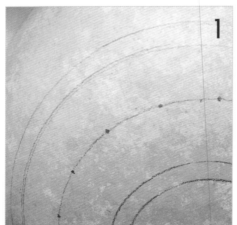

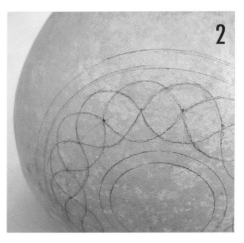

STEP FOUR: Erase the line on which the dots are drawn. Use the kneadable eraser and rub lightly and gently, taking care to not also erase the dots on the line.

STEP FIVE: Draw arches between dots. Starting with any dot, and skipping the one next to it, draw a moderate arch to the second dot in either direction (see photo 2). Draw arches both above and below the line on which the dots are drawn. Using the kneadable eraser, lift the top layer of graphite from the arch design, taking care to not erase the design completely.

STEP SIX: Broaden the arch design to ¼"–⅓"(see photo 3). Using the pencil and kneadable eraser, start overlapping arches to create the appearance of thick woven strands (see photo 4).

STEP SEVEN: Time to burn! Using a wood-burning tool with a standard or all-purpose tip on a medium setting, begin tracing all the lines drawn on the gourd, including the circular borders (see photo 5).

Tip:"The easiest way to make a nice even line is to set your pen on its narrow tip at the beginning of the line, and roll the gourd away from you, keeping the pen steady," Avery says. "If you need to work slower, then turn the heat down."

STEP EIGHT: Darken the negative areas around the braid. Continue with the moderate all-purpose tip on a wood-burning tool, but use the broader side of the tool instead of the narrow tip (see photo 6).

Note: Medium heat should be adequate to achieve a dark brown between braids. Avery cautions against getting overeager and turning up the heat; it's better to go over an area more than once than risk scorching the design.

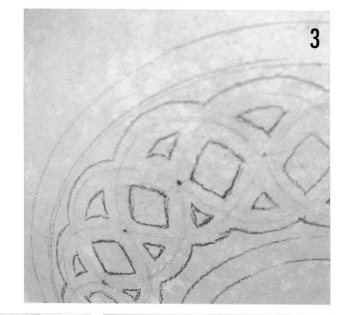

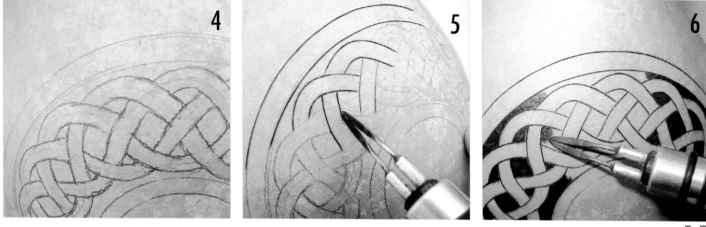

STEP NINE: Shade the areas where one strand passes under another. Using the shading tip on a wood-burning tool on medium heat, lightly touch the overlapping line at each crossover point and pull away from the line until satisfied with the level of shading (see photo 7). The goal is to create shadow where one strand would pass over another.

STEP TEN: Cut a hole for birds in the center of the design. Using a utility knife or drill, cut a hole in the center area of the design that will be removed. With a mini jigsaw, carefully cut along the drawn center circle and remove the gourd piece. Clean out the inside of the gourd with a long screwdriver (see page 11). Lightly sand the edge of the newly cut hole.

STEP ELEVEN: Paint the inside of the gourd. Using black acrylic craft paint and a long-handled narrow paintbrush, darken the gourd's interior, taking care to not get paint on the outside of the gourd.

Note: Of course, this birdhouse doesn't have to be inside. If it does serve as a legitimate home for avian friends, don't paint the inside of the gourd, drill several small holes in the base for drainage, and leave a few seeds in the bottom as an appetizer.

Tip: As an alternative, Avery suggests watering down the paint just a bit and "swishing it around inside of the gourd." Another alternative is to cover the gourd with a plastic shopping bag and tearing an opening in the bag through the hole in the gourd to apply paint. Be sure to tape the plastic in place (see photo 8).

STEP TWELVE: Apply color to the gourd if desired. For this piece, Avery uses a mahogany leather dye and carefully brushes on the color so as not to go into the border area around the Celtic design (see photo 9). The borders should retain their natural color. Allow the gourd to dry, then spray on a few coats of protective urethane, allowing each of those to dry fully between applications.

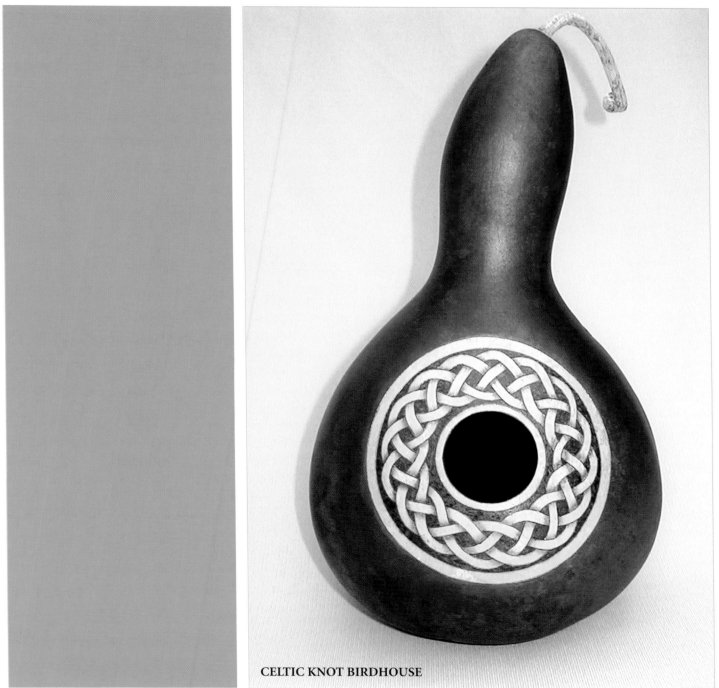

CELTIC KNOT BIRDHOUSE

Artist

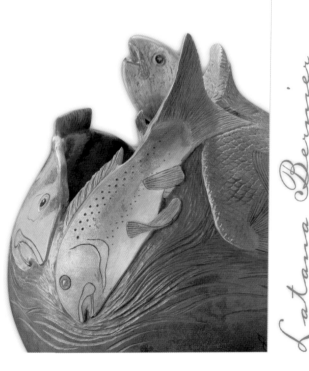

Latana Bernier

Trained in part by her father, a professor of fine art at St. Michael's College in Vermont, Latana Bernier recalls that when she shifted four years ago from clay sculpture to a focus on gourd art, he responded with, "Why are you messing around with those things! You should be sculpting!" These days, the professor prefers to remind his former pupil, "You know, Gauguin used to carve coconut shells."

From initial stages in which she basically used the gourd as a canvas, Bernier has developed a philosophy in which she "enlists the entire gourd in the formation of a kinetic sculptural piece." This approach is still very much informed by her training with clay sculpture with one obvious and significant difference: the gourd cannot actually be reshaped to achieve a particular form.

"All I can do is remove parts of the gourd to create the illusion of movement and flow. This is my current choice in rendering visually striking yet functionally viable gourd art." For Bernier, a small amount of inlay is the only acceptable material enhancement to the gourd in its natural state; she adds, "no other gourd scraps, no clay, nothing. If what I'm trying to create cannot be done within the physical limitations of the gourd, then I adapt my idea to fit the gourd." Her saving grace, she hastens to add, is that gourds exist in so many sizes and shapes. "I can always find one that allows mind and matter to meet!"

Bernier calls Virginia home and her primary commercial and artistic sphere is the mid-Atlantic region; but her work has also been displayed in galleries from Arizona to Maine. In the future, she is planning a move westward to Arizona, where Tom, her husband, will be privileged to take over full time as official "gourd cleaner."

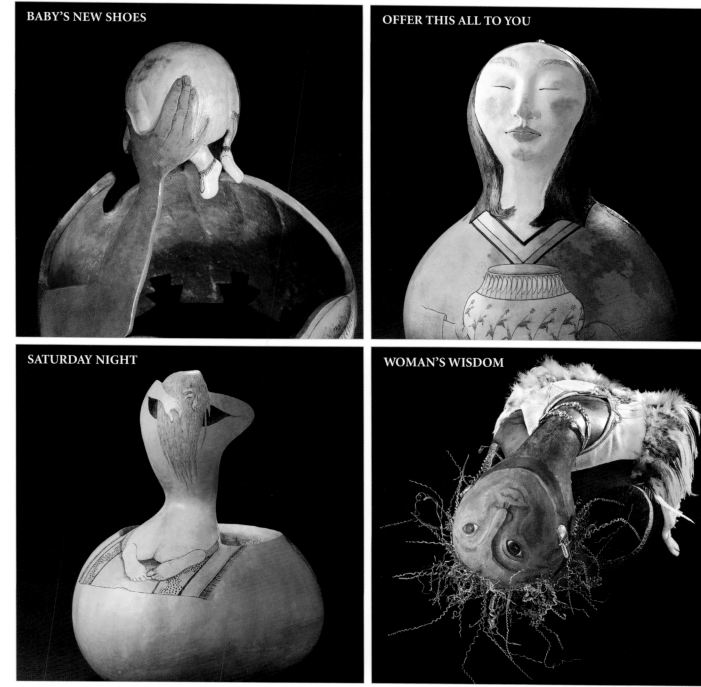

BABY'S NEW SHOES

OFFER THIS ALL TO YOU

SATURDAY NIGHT

WOMAN'S WISDOM

19

Project

BABY'S NEW SHOES

Everything about Bernier's philosophy and technique is evident in the piece pictured here, called Baby's New Shoes. While the following steps will technically illustrate how she accomplishes the final piece, they cannot identify how she first pictured the ultimate creation in an unaltered gourd. Each artist, Bernier says, has to find their own sources of inspiration—their own personal muse.

MATERIALS
• Acrylic paints: black, gray, white,
• Gilder's pastes: African bronze, sandalwood
• Glass seed beads
• Glue
• Gourd
• Heishi beads: coral
• Oil pencils: red, white
• Transparent glass paint: amber

TOOLS
• Drill or utility knife
• Hard-lead mechanical pencil
• Kneadable Eraser
• Mini jigsaw
• Paintbrushes
• Rotary tool with diamond bits: coarse, fine
• Sandpapers: fine grit, medium grit
• Soft-lead pencil or charcoal pencil
• Wood-burning system with various tips

STEP ONE: Clean the outside of the gourd (see page 9). Bernier starts Baby's New Shoes with a gourd roughly 15" tall and 13" across at its widest section. Develop a mental image of what you want to create and use a soft pencil or charcoal to sketch the design onto the outside of the gourd. "This stage is all trial and error, with erasing and redrawing coming rapidly as I attempt to conform my vision to the gourd's rigid anatomy," Bernier says. It might be helpful to sketch an initial design on paper before moving to the gourd.

STEP TWO: Cut away sections of the gourd to achieve the desired structure. Drill a hole or make a cut with a utility knife in the area of the gourd that will be cut away and removed, then use a mini jigsaw to create the basic shape of the finished piece by cutting along the sketched lines (see photo 1).

Note: For Bernier, the most effective jigsaw has a rounded rubber foot near the blade that allows her to get into every corner and niche effectively.

STEP THREE: With the basic shape established, use a rotary tool with a rounded diamond bit to create greater detail in baby's hands, arms, and head (see photo 2). Sand the inside of the gourd to clean it and prepare it for finishing.

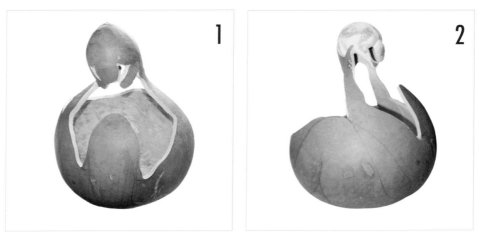

STEP FOUR: Bring baby more into focus. Draw mother's hands in specific detail, using your own hands as a visual guide. Pay particular attention to exactly where mother's hands end and baby begins. Using the rotary tool, remove the outer skin of the gourd everywhere that baby exists. Bernier carves to a depth ranging from ¹⁄₁₆" to ¼", and pays particular attention to anatomical detail "right down to the little bent fingers." Smooth out baby with fine sandpaper (see photos 3 and 4).

Tip: Bernier cautions against putting too much pressure on the gourd with the rotary tool as the surface is harder than the layer underneath. Let the tool do the work and "be patient." You may consider a larger bur-tip bit, but using the more efficient blade will also mean more sanding later to smooth out rough cuts. Touch up initial pencil sketches as they rub off throughout the process.

STEP FIVE: Using the mechanical pencil, draw baby's facial features very carefully in preparation for pyrography. Bernier advises paying special attention to the eyes, as anything that appears strange here will "make the entire piece off." Use foreshortening on a flat surface in drawing the face to give it a curved appearance.

STEP SIX: Using a wood-burning system with quality metal tips, burn Baby's features into the gourd surface (see photo 4). Bernier achieves most of the features, using a medium skew; but for darker areas, she uses a large ball tip. Be familiar with your wood-burning tool and test it out before actually using it on a piece.

STEP SEVEN: Using the mechanical pencil, focus on mother's hands, again using your own as a visual guide (see photo 5). Bernier recommends holding something in your own hands similar in shape to

what you are drawing as a more effective model. Use the wood-burning tool again with a medium skew to finish the hands, then proceed to mother's hair, strand by strand, using the same tool.

STEP EIGHT: Finish baby's feet and mother's headband. Bernier uses an oil pencil on baby's feet instead of acrylics for more muted color, and gives the infant white moccasins with red trim. Mother's feathers are white acrylic with gray acrylic shadowing, and the headband itself is a strip of coral heishi

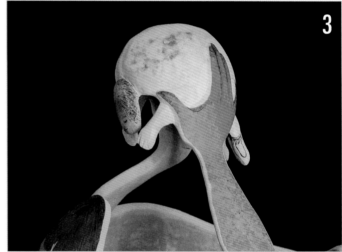

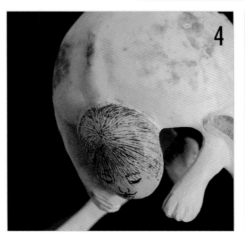

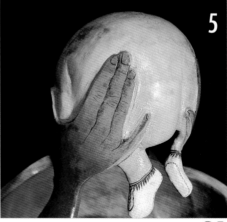

beads (see photo 6). To inlay the heishi, carve a strip only as wide as the beads and half as deep, then put a thin layer of glue in the bottom of the groove with a toothpick. Insert the beads and allow the glue a few minutes to dry. Using the exact same technique, Bernier also puts glass seed beads as accents around mother's moccasins (see photo 7).

STEP NINE: Bernier creates a pot between mother's knees and feet on the side of the gourd opposite her head. The pot is a combination of pyrography and carving, nothing more. Using the wood-burning tool, burn the outline of the pot, then give it depth by shading areas and designs (see photo 7). With the rotary tool, create additional accents by carving away the surface layer of the gourd to reveal the white underlayer.

STEP TEN: Finish the designs on the outside of the gourd. Using the wood-burning tool, pyrograph a Native American blanket design on the external bottom of the gourd and fill in the colors with oil pencil. Bernier a uses a Navajo design (see photo 7).

STEP ELEVEN: To give mother more definition and substance, color areas on the outside of the gourd around her arms and body. Bernier uses gilder's paste in African bronze for the green areas and sandalwood for the moccasins and leggings (see photos 6 and 7).

STEP TWELVE: Finish the inside of the gourd. Bernier recommends considering the theme of the gourd before choosing what to do with the inside. To call attention to the design on the outside, she uses an amber-colored transparent glass paint inside that almost perfectly matches the natural color of the gourd surface. She then paints in black acrylic a pattern onto the bottom inside of the bowl that matches the shape of the Navajo design on the outside and breaks up the open, interior space (see photo 8).

STEP THIRTEEN: With so much color both inside and outside the gourd, baby now appears stark and cold. To finish the piece, Bernier bathes baby in a wash created by diluting the amber transparent glass paint with water and applying it with a very soft brush. From this, baby receives depth and character, and no longer clashes with the rest of the finished piece.

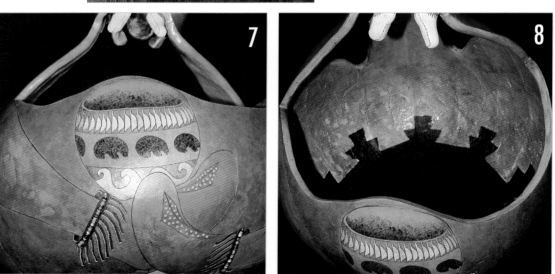

Rosalind Bonsett

In Somerset Maugham's early twentieth-century novel *The Moon and Sixpence*, a character named Charles Strickland abandons career and family to pursue painting with an all-consuming passion. Based on the life of Gauguin, Maugham's Strickland is a man who puts aside societal expectation for the purity of artistic obsession. Had he chosen art as his vocation in youth, maybe he would not have been devoured by it later in life.

Perhaps fortunately, Rosalind Bonsett discovered her love of art early on and incorporated it into her life. A graduate of the Minneapolis School of Art and Design, she also attended the Academia de Belle Arte in Florence. "My major was oil painting, which I continue to this day," she says, adding that, "my artwork has taken many turns."

In 1994, Bonsett was introduced to the gourd creations of Robert Rivera. "I was fascinated by the similarities to pottery without the attendant wheel, clay, kilns, and time," she recalls. "[Rivera's] use of natural color is a technique I still use."

From there, Bonsett's challenge became finding out more about gourds and how to acquire them. Research led her to the Indiana Gourd Society, then back to a local grower near her home in southern Indiana. "Through them, I became more involved in the gourd society and began seriously working on creating."

While she describes her earliest efforts as "fairly simple, with a Native American feel," in time Bonsett developed a signature style incorporating pen and ink drawing. "With time, I developed a more abstract design that is difficult to teach."

Yet teach Bonsett has, at annual gourd shows in Indiana. Over the past eight years, her distinctive work has won numerous ribbons and awards and has been sold and displayed in several galleries both in Indiana and her home state of Minnesota.

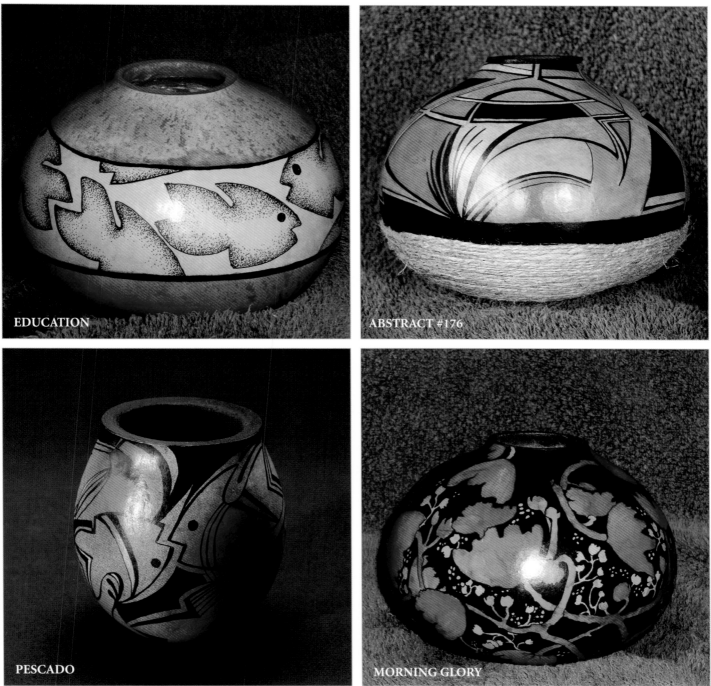

EDUCATION

ABSTRACT #176

PESCADO

MORNING GLORY

Project

PESCADO

While numerous gourd artists list Native American designs among their artistic influences, most are referring to the cultures of the American Southwest. Uniquely, one sees in Bonsett's designs the influence of more northern native cultures, most likely the result of where she lives. Also evident in her work is an attention to line direction and uses of space. "Using a stencil is the simplest way to demonstrate line direction and negative space," she says. Of course, the stencil is just the beginning, and the expansive remainder is filled with the Bonsett's unique abilities.

MATERIALS
• Gourd
• Spray paint: flat black
• Spray primer: rust
• Wax shoe polish: neutral

TOOLS
• Blue painter's tape
• Card stock for stencil
• Double-sided tape
• Mini jigsaw
• Pencil
• Permanent-ink technical pen: black
• Sandpaper: medium grit
• Tracing paper
• Utility knife

STEP ONE: Clean the outside of the gourd (see pages 8–11). For Pescado, Bonsett selects the top end of a Mexican bottle gourd. She cuts the gourd with a mini jigsaw to create what looks like a small gourd cup. In cutting the gourd, take care to ensure a straight clean cut and, hence, a level rim on the gourd (see photo 1). Clean the pulp and seeds out of the gourd and sand the interior and rim fairly smooth with medium-grit sandpaper.

STEP TWO: Paint the inside and the rim of the gourd. Using flat black spray paint, cover the inside of the gourd and the rim by spraying in short bursts to avoid runs and drips (see photo 2). Tape the outside, just beneath the rim of the gourd, to keep paint off the external areas, or "excess spray can be easily cleaned off with lacquer thinner," Bonsett says. Let the paint dry completely, and add additional coats if necessary.

STEP THREE: Add color to the outside of the gourd. The goal here is not to paint the entire outside surface, but instead to create splashes of color around the gourd. Using rust-colored spray primer, apply "random spurts" here and there, "keeping the natural gourd color open in places" (see photo 3). To keep the rust-colored paint off the black area, it would be a good idea to tape the rim of the gourd.

STEP FOUR: Create a stencil from card stock. For Pescado, Bonsett draws a simple but somewhat abstract fish design as shown in Diagram A, then cuts it out. The swirls and splashes incorporated in the final piece work well with the fish design, and Bonsett encourages others to consider the final design in determining what kind of stencil to create.

STEP FIVE: Apply the stencil design to the gourd. Double-sided tape will probably help a great deal with this step in the process. Simply tape the stencil to the gourd and trace around it (see photo 4). "Keep in mind the different areas of color and try to highlight those areas with your stencil line," Bonsett advises. "Trace another outline near the first, but in another direction." Continue this tracing process until the desired number of outlines is applied to the gourd. Keep in mind the ultimate creative goal in choosing where to trace.

STEP SIX: Connect the outlines on the gourd. For this, the most freely creative part of the process, Bonsett uses a permanent-ink technical pen and "connects the shapes with lines, being aware of negative spaces. Be creative with thick and thin lines and interesting shapes, keeping in mind your basic outlines" (see photo 5).

STEP SEVEN: Protect the finished piece. When completed, Bonsett prefers to cover the entire piece with a neutral wax shoe polish, let it set, and then buff to a soft shine.

DIAGRAM A

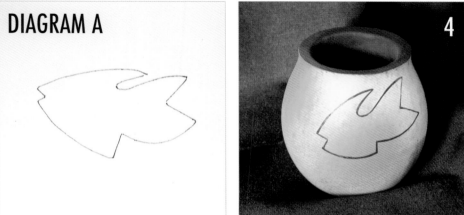

Artist

Carla Bratt

Imagine for a moment that you have a favorite gadget, electronic or otherwise. This item has attractive features and you love it, but there is lacking a certain passion, an intimacy. On a particular occasion, you receive as a gift another gadget so versatile that you can never exhaust its capabilities. You are smitten, irrevocably enthralled.

As Carla Bratt remembers it, artistic endeavors had always played a role in her life, but none could compare with the "intimate love affair" she developed with gourds. Eighteen years ago, they became the ideal gadget, valued for their "infinite numbers of shapes and sizes; their complex curves, smooth surfaces and golden glows." In gourds, Bratt found an endless number of creative possibilities—the romance was cemented.

"Cutting, carving, burning, painting, embellishing, and weaving—over the years I've employed countless techniques on gourds, all self-taught and some even self-invented," Bratt says. It's clearly a reciprocal relationship—the gourds inspire and she creates.

A substantial part of Bratt's inspiration comes from "explosive epiphanies" about the natural world, which might lead her to craft pieces reflecting "a Navajo rug, or the sea on a stormy day." She then uses mixed media—"a splash of color, the smoothness of polished abalone, the flash of a bird's feather"—to create an inspired finished piece.

From initially creating gourds as personal gifts, Bratt moved into the "greater world of retail art." Currently showing in West Coast galleries and stores, even she is a bit surprised at where these simple squash have taken her. "It has been such a long and rewarding process. Along the way, I have discovered myself, acquired lifelong friends, and learned to look at life's never-ending connections and reconnections."

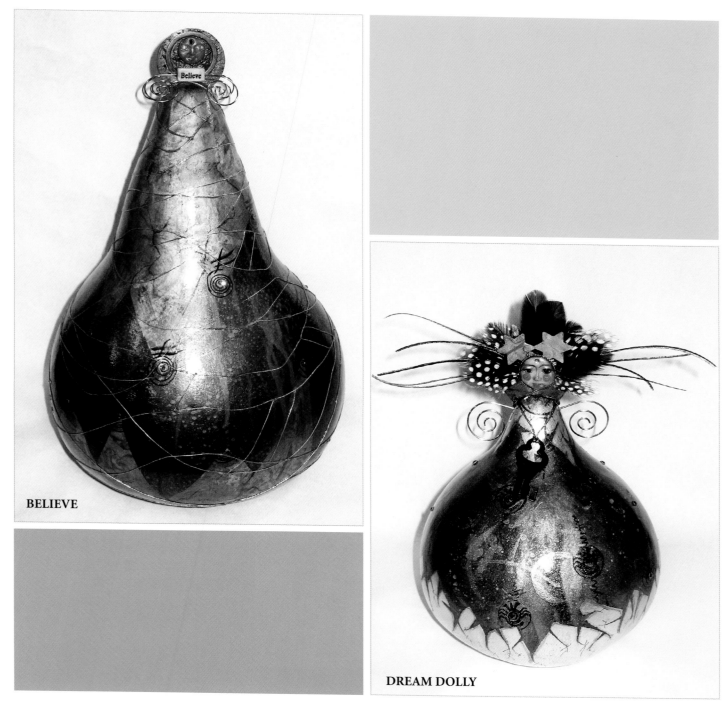

BELIEVE

DREAM DOLLY

Project

ASIAN DRAGONS

How, exactly, to define Bratt's work? At the center of each piece is pyroengraving, painting and/or foiling, and to that she adds a healthy dose of her own creative intellect and techniques borrowed from collage work, photography, and printing. The result is an "artistic journey" that, through experimentation, has enabled her to understand well a gourd's capabilities.

MATERIALS
- Acrylic paints: metallic gold, metallic plum
- Acrylic spray sealer: matte finish
- Alcohol inks: deep blue, forest green, purple, turquoise
- Antiquing varnish
- Beading thread: #18 black
- Embellishments: (2) ¾" carved ivory disks (flat on one side), (8) 1" brass Chinese coin, (2) crystals (flat on one side), (6) ivory beads, (16) small black beads
- Foil: 6–8 sheets, blue or green variegated
- Foil adhesive
- Gourd
- Industrial-strength craft adhesive
- Isopropyl rubbing alcohol
- Metal disk: 2" diameter, 24 gauge
- Pinpoint precision glue
- Wood putty

TOOLS
- Cotton balls
- Cotton swabs
- Crafter's heat-embossing tool
- Flexible ruler
- Foil burnishing tool or metal spoon
- Hacksaw (if necessary)
- Hand file (if necessary)
- Paper towels
- Pencil and eraser
- Plastic spray bottles (6 total): (5) 4 oz., 8 oz.
- Pruning shears
- Rotary tool with cutting, drilling, and sanding bits
- Sable brushes: #6 round, 1" flat
- Sponge
- Steel wool: #0000 superfine, (2 packages)
- Tack cloth
- Wooden craft sticks

STEP ONE: Clean the exterior of the gourd (see page 9). Use pruning shears to snip off the gourd stem. For this project, Bratt selects a pear-shaped gourd roughly 15" tall and 30" around at its widest point.

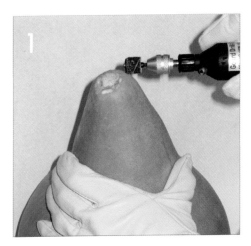

STEP TWO: Prepare stem area of gourd. Attach a sanding tip to a rotary tool and sand smooth the area where the stem of the gourd was (see photo 1). Identify a front and back of the gourd and draw a horizontal line on the top center of the gourd, separating the two sides. A flexible ruler will be helpful in drawing a line on top of the gourd.

STEP THREE: Cut a slit in the top of the gourd. Switch the sanding tip on the rotary tool to a cutting tip and begin cutting along the line drawn on the top of the gourd (see photo 2). The slit will hold the 24-gauge 2" metal disk. Pause periodically and slide the disk into the slit to check the fit.

Note: The disk fits the way it should when it goes in deep enough to retain upright stability. Bratt says it may be necessary to use a small hacksaw or hand file to make the slit wide and deep enough for the disk, and that artists should not worry "if the slit seems too long at this point."

STEP FOUR: Wipe the gourd with the tack cloth. Dip a cotton ball in rubbing alcohol and use it to wipe clean the surface of the gourd.

STEP FIVE: Using a craft stick, apply wood putty to the slit in the top of the gourd and wipe off excess with a damp rag or paper towel. Slide the disk into the slit and press firmly, then stabilize the disk by applying more putty around it and wiping off excess (see photo 3). Make sure to fill in any part of the slit not utilized by the disk. The slit should not be visible at all in the finished piece. Let the wood putty dry overnight.

Tip: Bratt sometimes uses a heat (embossing) tool to hasten the drying process so she can continue working on a piece the same day.

STEP SIX: Check disk very gently when putty is dry to see that it is solidly in place. Using fine-grit sandpaper and #0000 steel wool, remove any excess putty to create a smooth surface even with that of the gourd. Repeat cleaning process with tack cloth and rubbing alcohol.

STEP SEVEN: Paint the entire gourd with metallic acrylic paint. In creating this piece, Bratt chooses a metallic plum acrylic (see photo 4). Apply three coats of paint, allowing each coat to dry before lightly rubbing it with #0000 steel wool and wiping with the tack cloth. For this project, Bratt uses a 1"-wide flat sable brush.

Note: The drying process can be sped up through use of the heat tool.

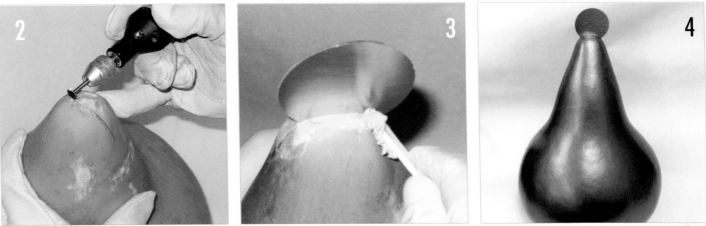

STEP EIGHT: Put alcohol inks in spray bottles for application. Put 1 oz. of each color chosen in four of the 4 oz. spray bottles; dilute each color with ½ oz. of rubbing alcohol. For this piece, Bratt chooses deep blue, forest green, purple, and turquoise. Fill the fifth 4 oz. spray bottle with 1 oz. of metallic acrylic paint and dilute with 1–2 oz. of water. Bratt chooses warm metallic gold. Fill the 8 oz. bottle with rubbing alcohol.

Tip: Bratt warns against overdiluting the paints when mixing in spray bottles. "The paint should spray easily, but not be runny."

STEP NINE: Apply inks to the gourd. Set the gourd on a pedestal in an area where it is safe to spray, and stand 12"–24" away (see photo 5). Spray alcohol inks lightly and randomly on the gourd, balancing the colors applied. Use caution with darker inks as they are more intense in color.

STEP TEN: Spray rubbing alcohol over inked gourd. The more alcohol you spray over the gourd, the more diluted the inks will become, so spray cautiously at first and observe the results. Rotate the gourd and turn it upside down to blend colors and cause streaks and designs. As this is not a strictly defined process, Bratt says to "let your imagination control the color process." Stop running or dripping using the heat tool on a particular area.

Note: This stage of the process, Bratt says, "is very quick, usually not exceeding ten or fifteen minutes." Additional effects can be created using an alcohol-dampened sponge. Dry the surface of the gourd with the heat tool when satisfied with the results, but be very careful not to scorch or bubble the applied ink.

STEP ELEVEN: Spray metallic acrylic paint on gourd "in a random yet balanced pattern. Paint should have a 'spattered' effect," Bratt says (see photo 6). Let paint dry.

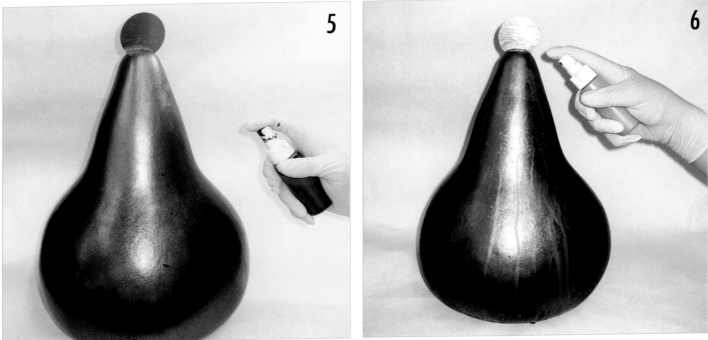

STEP TWELVE: Use foiling to enhance the gourd's appearance. The placement of the foil is best left to the discretion of the artist. First, using a #6 round sable brush, apply foil adhesive to the gourd surface and the metal disk. Bratt applies foil to the top third of the gourd—including the disk—and leaves the bottom foil line uneven (see photo 7). The adhesive should be applied in thin layers and allowed to dry to a clear sheen before the foil is applied. Gently press the foil into place, then burnish it with a burnishing tool or the back of a metal spoon. In this example, Bratt also uses #0000 steel wool to give the foil a more "distressed" look.

STEP THIRTEEN: Add decorative calligraphic elements. Using black acrylic paint and a round sable brush (or a calligraphic brush), Bratt paints Chinese- or Japanese-looking characters randomly all the way around the gourd. For help with this, look at a book on Chinese or Japanese language.

STEP FOURTEEN: After drying, use a sealer to protect the gourd's surface. Bratt first sprays on a matte sealer and then finishes by brushing on an antique varnish. Let the sealer dry completely before adding the final embellishments.

STEP FIFTEEN: Drill two holes in the metallic disk for decorating (see photo 8). The holes should be just above the two points where the disk connects with the gourd.

STEP SIXTEEN: Decorate the foiled metallic disk. Bratt chooses matching carved ivory disks with an Asian theme and attaches one to each side, using an industrial-strength adhesive. She also adds a crystal to the forehead of each disk as an extra touch.

STEP SEVENTEEN: The embellishment continues! For added flare, Bratt ties Asian-themed beads and coins onto black thread and attaches the strings of items through the holes in the metallic disk (see photos 8 and 9). She also recommends applying a single dot of pinpoint precision glue to each knot to prevent unraveling.

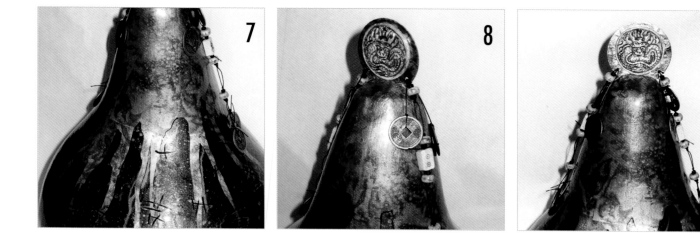

Artist

Karen Brown

In the fairy tale, Jack acquires a handful of magic beans that his mother angrily throws into the yard before sending young Jack off to bed. In the morning, the beans have grown into a huge stalk leading to a magical land of giants, gold-producing poultry, and a crooning stringed instrument. From the beans, Jack acquires fortune and happiness.

In 1998, Karen Brown acquired a packet of gourd seeds and planted them in the yard. The following morning, there were only the covered holes where the gourds had been planted—no golden eggs, no singing harp, no big people. Months later, however, Brown finally received her reward in the form of approximately thirty gourds. The problem was, she didn't know what to do with them.

"When I found out it would take almost six months for the green gourds to dry out, I requested all the books the library system had on hand and a few they ordered from out-of-town libraries," Brown explains. When one gourd dried sufficiently, she made her first piece, a simple bowl. "I knew I'd found my calling."

Indeed. Her enthusiasm expanding rapidly, Brown went to her first gourd show in 2001, entered thirty-six pieces, and left with twenty-two ribbons. Not just a calling, gourd arts constitute a community in which she is respected and comfortable. Gourd shows remind Brown "of the county fairs of my youth."

Raised in rural southern Michigan and initially educated in a one-room schoolhouse, gourds are an artistic connection to the natural environment and pastoral existence Brown so enjoys. Trained for a year and a half at the Kendal School of Art and Design in Grand Rapids, Michigan. She left because "I found traditional art very restrictive." From there, she did commissioned work for several years before the fateful arrival of the seeds.

A member of the Indiana and American Gourd Societies, and Gourd Artist Guild online group, Brown lives in Alaska, Michigan, with husband Mark and three cats. Her work is displayed in local galleries, jewelry stores, and garden centers.

A MAPLE IN FALL

A GOURDBERRY TREE

Wonderfully, this particular piece combines two of Brown's passions: gourds and trees. Even better, it does so in a piece with great beauty and utility. The result of concerted prior experimentation, the Gourdberry Tree is not an easy project. However, it offers the promise of so much self-satisfaction at the conclusion that it's hard to pass up.

MATERIALS
- Acrylic paints: black, three shades of brown and of green (dark, medium, light), Italian Red for basecoat
- Blended fibers texture gel: medium
- Brass disk: 2"–4" diameter (depending on trunk) with ½" hole
- Brass finial for top of shade
- Brass nuts and washers: (2 each) for threaded rod
- Electric cord with plug on one end
- Gold leafing: (10) sheets or more (depending on size of shade)
- Gourds: large canteen, long dipper
- Leafing adhesive
- Light fixture with 2 parallel sockets and pull chains
- Lightbulbs: (2) 40-watt maximum
- Mahogany, walnut, or other hardwood piece: at least 12" square and ¾" thick
- Paint pen: black or greenish brown, extra fine
- Polyacrylic varnish: satin finish
- Polyurethane: satin finish
- Threaded rods: 36" x ½", 1"–2" x ¼" (if necessary)
- Wood stain: dark walnut

TOOLS
- Drill or drill press with ¼" and ½" bits
- Hand files: small
- Hard-lead mechanical pencil
- Latex gloves
- Leaf template
- Mini jigsaw
- Paintbrushes: #000 or liner, #0–#2 rounds, varnish brush
- Palette knife: narrow
- Rotary tool with grout removal bit, flap wheel, small- and medium-ball bur bits, large-cone grinding stone, long fine-cone grinding stone, cutting disk, sanding drum, U gouge (optional)
- Sandpapers: 100, 200, and 400 grits
- Steel wool: #000
- Stencil brush: large round
- Tack cloth
- Tweezers
- Utility knife or awl
- Wire cutters with wire strippers for wiring light fixture

STEP ONE: Clean the outside of the two gourds (see page 9).

Note: More than most other projects, the selection of gourds is very important here. The canteen gourd, Brown says, needs to be big enough to hide parts of the lamp (lightbulbs, etc.); the dipper gourd needs to be as straight as possible. Exactly how long the dipper should be depends on the size of the canteen. "Keep the trunk in proportion with the overall look of the design," Brown says, "and don't be afraid to turn a few gourds over" in selecting them.

STEP TWO: Turn the dipper gourd into a tree trunk. First, make a mark on the bulb end so that cutting it off will leave a bit of flare to act as "roots" on the tree; make a similar mark on the other end of the gourd, based on how high you want to trunk to be. The trunk section should be about 36" long to cover the threaded rod. Make a hole near the lines on both ends of the gourd with a utility knife or awl. Insert the mini jigsaw and cut the ends off along the lines drawn around the gourd, making sure to cut the ends as straight as possible. Sand the flared end so that the "trunk" stands up straight. Sand the top end and clean the pulp and seeds out of the gourd. Because the inside of the dipper will never be visible, Brown says it isn't necessary to be obsessive about cleaning out the gourd. As a final step, score the flared end of the trunk to create the appearance of gnarled roots, using a rotary tool with a sanding drum (see photo 1).

STEP THREE: Give color and texture to the trunk. First, mix medium brown acrylic paint with texture gel to create $\frac{1}{2}-\frac{3}{4}$ cup of material. Apply this to the dipper gourd with a palette knife, giving the trunk lots of texture. When satisfied with the texture, let the trunk dry for a few days, then go back and add darker and lighter brown highlights to "give the trunk more visual interest," Brown says. "Check out some real trees for the type of bark you like best."

STEP FOUR: Draw a line around the bottom of the canteen gourd for the shade. Brown first determines visually how far down she wants the shade to fall, then simply draws a line around the gourd. It might be helpful to measure down from the center of the bottom part of the gourd and make marks in equal increments around the gourd so that the line for the shade is straight. "Step back and take a look to see if the line is low enough on the gourd," Brown says. "As long as it's deep enough to hide the lamp parts," it should be fine.

STEP FIVE: Apply the leaf pattern to the area of the gourd that will be the shade (see photo 2). Brown has several different sizes of posterboard leaf templates she uses, and suggests that templates could come from the leaves of plants around the house, books, or freehand drawings. While mixing two or three sizes creates a more diverse and interesting pattern, for this project Brown sticks with just one size template. Using one template with a bit of masking tape on the back, Brown says, "I always start at the center of the top, sketching four or five leaves around the center of the piece." She traces the leaf, then moves it to an empty space, continuing this process until the entire shade is covered with traced leaf patterns down to the penciled line. It's okay if some hang over the line. "Leave some blank spaces around your leaves," Brown says. "These will be cut out later and allow the golden glow from the lamp to come shining through."

STEP SIX: Cut away the shade from the bottom of the canteen gourd. Using the awl or utility knife, make a hole beneath the line marked for the bottom of the shade. Insert the mini jigsaw and cut the shade away from the rest of the gourd, carefully cutting around leaves where necessary. "This is an exciting cut to make," Brown says, "separating the shade." When it is completely separate, scrape the pulp and seeds out completely, then sand the inside of the shade well. "Start with an 80-grit flap wheel on a rotary tool, then use 100-grit sandpaper, and work your way up to 400-grit for that smooth-as-glass feel."

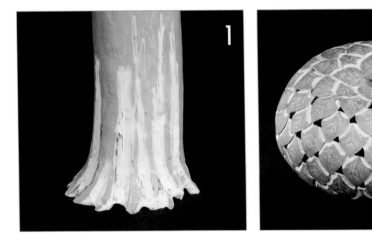

STEP SEVEN: Begin to structure and form the leaf shade. First, punch holes in the shade everywhere there are gaps in the foliage, using the awl or utility knife. Use the jigsaw to carve out all these small areas around the leaves. It may be necessary to use a rotary tool with a grout-removal bit if the gourd is too thick. "When all these little 'puzzle pieces' are out, you can begin to carve the leaves," Brown says. Using a rotary tool with a medium-ball bur bit, start to follow the outline of each leaf so that it should appear as on top of another. Start at the top and work down. "Some leaves will only need you to carve out the tips that hang over the leaves below them," she says. "Others will have almost the entire leaf carved away from the leaf below it."

Tip: Brown advises "going easy while removing material from the shade. You can always remove more—you just can't put back what you carved away. As you continue to work, you'll be going back over these leaves several times. You can also use a U gouge to do this first cutting. Gouge out the leaf edges, then go back in with the rotary tool to cut away more of the leaves."

STEP EIGHT: Add detail to the leaves in the shade. Brown switches to a small-ball bur bit on the rotary tool to "undercut each leaf and show more depth. This requires a steady hand and

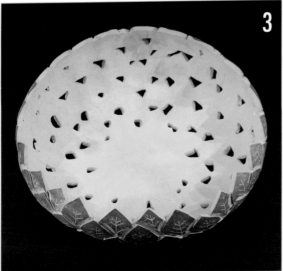

3

a lot of time, but it will really bring your leaves to life." Use the same small bit to cut veins in the leaves, then switch to a long fine-cone grinding stone to create a gentle slope on each leaf from center to edge, as leaves would naturally appear.

STEP NINE: Sand the holes in the shade to make them a bit wider. From the inside of the shade (see photo 3), Brown uses a large-cone grinding stone on the rotary tool and gradually widens the holes to permit "more light to come through the shade." Be careful not to cut into the leaves on the upper side of the shade. She then takes the small files and smoothes out all of the rough edges, rough spots, and machine marks on both sides of the gourd. "I go over and over my shade to make sure I didn't miss any spots." Blow all the dust and gourd bits off the shade. Brown uses the blow function of her vacuum cleaner.

STEP TEN: Paint the underside of the shade with polyacrylic varnish. Keep the varnish from running through the holes onto the leaves on the top side, and wash it off quickly with a damp cloth if any does sneak through. The varnish cleans up easily with soap and water, but also will give the underside of the gourd a grainy texture. When dry, sand the varnish with #000 steel wool or 400-grit sandpaper, then wipe clean with a tack cloth. Brown says two coats of varnish, with sanding after each is dry, may be necessary to "bring the shade back to a smooth feel again."

STEP ELEVEN: Paint the shade. Brown first paints the underside of the shade with an Italian Red basecoat and allows it to dry overnight (see photo 4). Next, she paints the inside of each hole and the outside edge of each leaf with black acrylic and allows that to dry. Finally, she paints the leaves (see photo 5), starting with those on top and working with a palette of a few different shades of green. "I like to start with darkest green at the back of the leaves that would be shaded by others, then mix lighter shades farther out on the leaves as I move down the shade." Toward the bottom, Brown sets the shade on craft paper or newspaper so as to turn it without touching the paint.

STEP TWELVE: If a steady hand is not a concern, mix dark green with dark brown or black and paint the veins on the leaves with a fine-tipped brush (see photo 6). If maintaining a steady hand seems frightening, Brown says an extra-fine paint pen will do the trick. Let the shade dry overnight.

STEP THIRTEEN: Brush leafing adhesive on the underside of the shade. "Treat this stuff like leather dye," Brown advises, "very little on the brush when applying it to the gourd. If it happens to run through the holes, wipe it off the leaves with a damp rag." Apply two coats, letting each dry overnight in between, to ensure the whole thing is covered and the gold leafing will stick.

STEP FOURTEEN: Apply gold leafing to the underside of the shade. "Admittedly," Brown says, "this is a tedious and trouble-some process." She wears latex gloves and picks up each sheet with tweezers, laying it gently into the concave underside of the shade. She then taps the sheet gently into place with a stencil brush. Overlap the sheets by about ¼", and when all are laid down and placed correctly, "softly swirl the brush around and rub off the excess leafing." Push the leafing through the holes in the shade, and gently rub all leafing off areas without adhesive and where the sheets overlap—wherever there is no adhesive, the leafing should rub off with gentle brushing. Use the scraps that come off to touch up spots that need it.

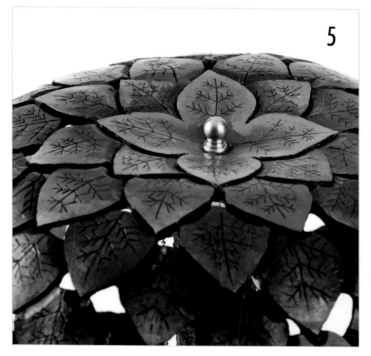

STEP FIFTEEN: Seal the shade and the trunk with polyurethane. Apply two or three coats to the shade, letting each dry to the touch before sanding lightly with #000 steel wool and wiping with the tack cloth. "Don't rush this step," Brown advises. "You don't want to create a great lamp, only to not have the finish right. Be sure to check for runs in the finish." Don't bother trying to sand the trunk, given the texture. Allow both the trunk and the shade to dry completely.

STEP SIXTEEN: Create the base for the lamp. Brown prefers sturdy hardwoods like mahogany or walnut, and tries to pick up quality scraps from local furniture makers. The base only needs to be big enough to support the weight of the lamp and keep it stable. Use a compass to draw a 12"-diameter circle on the board (the size of the base can vary based on lamp height). Cut out the base, route the edge with a half-round bit, and sand it smooth. Use a drill press to create a ½" hole in the center of the base for the threaded rod. Turn the base over and rout a ¼" furrow from the center hole to the edge for the power cord. Using the same ¼" bit, rout a larger center hole on the underside of the base only for the nut that will be attached to the threaded rod. Finally, Brown prefers to stain the base with dark walnut stain, let it dry, then brush on two or three coats of polyurethane. Again, let the finish dry and sand lightly with #000 steel wool or 400-grit sandpaper before wiping with a tack cloth and applying the next coat.

STEP SEVENTEEN: Drill a ¼" hole in the center of the shade. Brown puts the shade on a piece of scrap wood and drills from the inside out to create a clean hole on the upper side of the shade.

STEP EIGHTEEN: Begin to assemble the lamp. Using a brass washer and nut, bolt the threaded rod to the base, and place the trunk piece over the rod so that it protrudes from the top of the trunk. Hold the light fixture up to the top of the rod and estimate where to cut the rod. Brown finds the best place is usually about ½" above the top of the trunk. Using the rotary tool and cutting disk, cut off the end of the rod at the established mark. Depending on the length of the rod, it may be necessary to rethread the top. Glue the trunk down to the base, thread the brass disk with the ½" hole in the middle onto the rod to cover the top of the trunk, then lock the disk down with a washer and nut.

STEP NINETEEN: Finish assembling the lamp. Thread the power cord up through the rod and wire it to the light fixture; cover bare threaded wires with electrical tape. Screw the light fixture onto the top of the rod and make it snug with the nut holding the brass disk to the top of the trunk. Attach the shade to the light fixture and secure it with a brass finial. Brown says that, "some light fixtures will require you to get a 1"-long piece of ¼" threaded rod to thread the finial onto. Other fixtures will include this piece. Depending on the thickness of your shade, you may have to get a longer piece of ¼" threaded rod to make the shade fit."

THE GOURDBERRY TREE

Artist

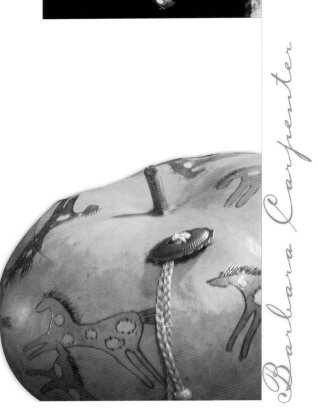

Barbara Carpenter

Art has been a part of Barbara Carpenter's life since "she received her first box of crayons," she recalls now. And while she made a conscious effort to keep it in her life by painting in traditional mediums, "something was still missing."

Carpenter toyed with the idea of pottery but was dissuaded by the thought of working with a kiln at her Mesa, Arizona, home. In the midst of this artistic pilgrimage, she attended a woodcarving show and for the first time came upon gourd artists. "Wow! Here was ready-made pottery waiting to be decorated and embellished," Carpenter recalls. The search for a medium was over.

She purchased her first gourds that day, and within forty-eight hours had created the piece explained here. From the initial attraction to gourds for their "ready-made pottery" qualities, Carpenter has grown to also appreciate their distinctiveness. "The gourds provide canvases that are as individual and unique as the people who acquire them."

Arguably, gourds were simply the culmination of a creative awakening. Before becoming "addicted to gourds," Carpenter earned degrees in marketing, business administration, digital animation and production. She now uses those talents to promote her craft, as well as the history of gourds. Much of that information is shared through gourd art classes Carpenter teaches locally.

While gourds are not exclusive to the Southwest, there does seem to be a connection between region and craft. For Carpenter, a Pittsburgh native, the beauty of the Sonoran desert convinced her to move to Arizona in 1986. The desert landscape gave her the opportunity to find gourds as a medium, and provides still the inspiration for her work.

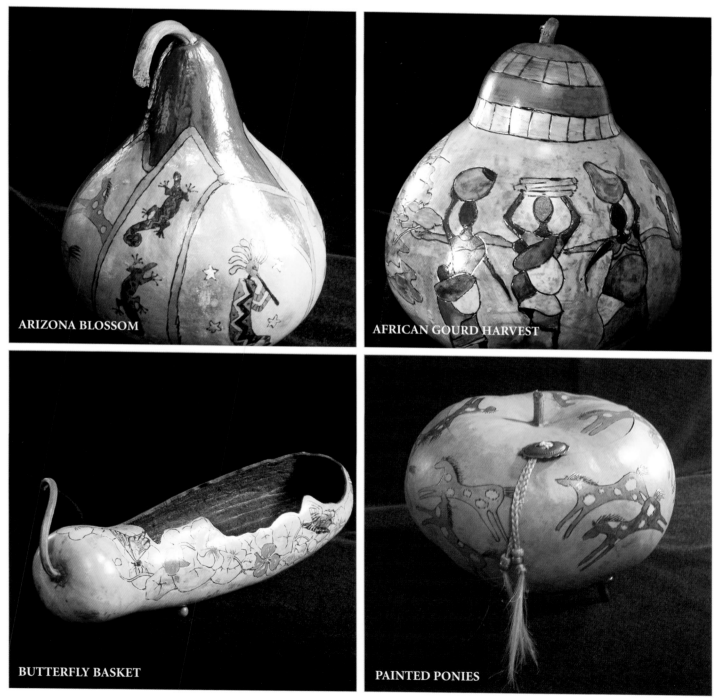

ARIZONA BLOSSOM

AFRICAN GOURD HARVEST

BUTTERFLY BASKET

PAINTED PONIES

43

HOLDING THE PAST TOGETHER

This particular piece seems very much inspired by Carpenter's home. Clearly evident are the Sonoran desert in the lizard design and any number of native Southwestern cultures in the idea of broken pottery shards. Albeit, where she really succeeds is in giving this piece a modern look and striking appearance in the use of metallic acrylic paints. The radiance of the finish is captivating.

MATERIALS
• Acrylic paints, 2 oz. bottles: black, brick, tan, terra-cotta, white
• Acrylic spray paint: flat black
• Acrylic spray sealer: matte finish
• Gourd
• Metallic acrylic craft paints, 2 oz. bottles: black pearl, champagne gold, emperor's gold, royal ruby
• Permanent marker: black, fine tip

TOOLS
• Acetone nail polish remover
• Blue painter's tape
• Cotton balls and swabs
• Eraser
• Graphite sketching pencil
• Lizard outline of choice on heavy paper (several poses are best)
• Mini jigsaw
• Paintbrushes: assorted small
• Plastic grocery bag

• Transfer paper (unwaxed)
• Utility knife
• Wood-burning tool with all-purpose tip

STEP ONE: Clean the surface of the gourd (see page 9). For this project, Carpenter picks a medium-sized bottle or flat rounded gourd.

STEP TWO: Pencil a rough, uneven line on the neck of the gourd just where it starts to flare out toward the stem. This will give the finished piece a bit of a lip. With a utility knife, cut through the gourd at a point on the line drawn in pencil and make an incision deep enough to get the blade of a mini jigsaw through.

STEP THREE: Cut off the top of the gourd. Use the mini jigsaw and follow the pencil line around the neck of the gourd until the top comes free. "This does not have to be perfect," Carpenter says. "The more jagged looking, the better the results" (see photo 1).

Tip: For protection and security, Carpenter recommends using a pillow or piece of leather under the gourd on your lap while you cut. She also says some sort of nonslip gloves for holding the gourd while you cut are a good and safe idea.

STEP FOUR: Clean the inside of the gourd and let it dry thoroughly (see page 9).

STEP FIVE: Paint the inside of the gourd. Place the gourd inside the plastic grocery sack and gather the bag as close as possible around the rim of the gourd. Using the blue painter's tape, secure the bag to the outside of the gourd and extend the tape above the rim of the gourd without it actually sticking to the rim (see photo 2). Press tape tightly to the gourd to avoid paint overspraying onto the exterior. Spray the inside of the gourd black with the flat black acrylic. Carpenter advises against trying to cover the inside in one application. "Apply several light coats and let them dry in between." Carefully remove the tape and bag when the last coat is dry.

STEP SIX: On the widest part of the gourd, use the blue painter's tape to attach the lizard design over the transfer paper (see photo 3). Start to trace around the lizard lightly, then lift the paper and make sure the design is transferring satisfactorily. Finish tracing around the lizard with a "light touch. A light touch is easier to erase and move in case you change your mind," Carpenter says.

Tip: Carpenter created her lizard design by studying lizards in her own backyard. For those not inclined to freehand talent, she recommends a child's coloring book on reptiles, library books, or perhaps a Web site.

STEP SEVEN: Add more lizards! Repeat the process with the lizard design and transfer paper until the gourd has connecting lizards all over it. Carpenter slightly overlaps her lizards—"a foot touching a tail, maybe"—and plays with the patterns, turning them upside down or at an angle. When finished with the lizard design, erase any unnecessary pencil lines, paying special attention to the areas that overlap.

Note: When working with larger gourds, Carpenter draws inside each lizard design a second line approximately ¼" from the first, giving the outlines a broad frame. "This creates a stripe that I then color in black when it is time to paint. This really 'pops' the lizards by accentuating them."

STEP EIGHT: Draw "broken pottery" lines on the gourd. Carpenter pencils in random lines that form a patchwork between the lizards. She recommends creating different shapes and sizes for interesting effect, and making sure the lines go all the way to the bottom of the gourd. "It is best to have the lizards partially lying over two or more pieces at a time. This is what makes it look like they are holding all the pieces together"

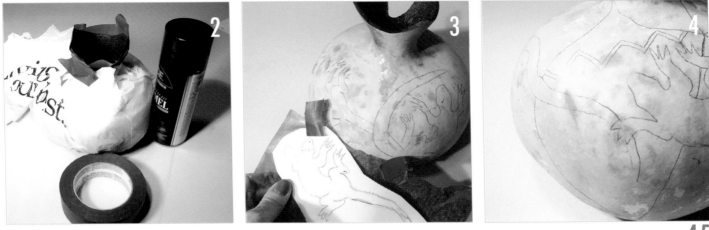

(see photo 4). To complete the sketch, draw some "Ancient Pottery"-type designs inside approximately a third of the pieces. "Don't make it look too busy."

STEP NINE: Burn the lizard and pottery designs into the gourd. Using a wood-burning tool with an all-purpose tip and moderate heat, burn the outline of the lizards first. Move to the outlines of the pottery pieces and make them darker and deeper by "pressing harder and moving slowly. This gives the piece depth and makes the gourd look more authentic," Carpenter explains. Be careful to apply just the right pressure and not burn through the gourd. Finally, use a light touch to finish with the "Ancient Pottery" design elements (see photo 5).

STEP TEN: Paint the various pottery pieces first. Using the nonmetallic acrylics, paint each of the pottery pieces, taking care to vary the colors and not use the same color in adjoining pieces (see photo 6). To create a consistent, bold image, Carpenter applies several coats of paint, letting each dry before applying another. Next, use varying colors to fill in the "Ancient

Pottery" design elements, also using several coats if needed. If mistakes are made, clean them up with cotton balls and/or swabs and acetone nail polish remover.

STEP ELEVEN: Give the lizards some color! Using different metallic acrylics, paint each of the lizards a different color. Be patient! Carpenter says the metallic paints are a bit harder to work with, and "take more coats and time to get smooth."

Note: As mentioned in the note after Step Seven on page 45, Carpenter creates a thick border around the lizards on large gourds that she then fills in with black acrylic. On smaller gourds, she goes back (if necessary) after the paint is completely dry and redefines the outline of the pottery and lizards with a fine-tipped permanent black marker.

STEP TWELVE: Protect your work. After the paint is completely dry, Carpenter shakes vigorously a can of clear acrylic sealer. Then, holding the can at least 12" away, she sprays it on the gourd. To cover the gourd top and bottom, invert it over a stand of some sort. Carpenter advises several light coats of clear acrylic instead of one heavy coat (see photo 7). Allow drying between each. "Don't forget to sign your work of art!" she recommends.

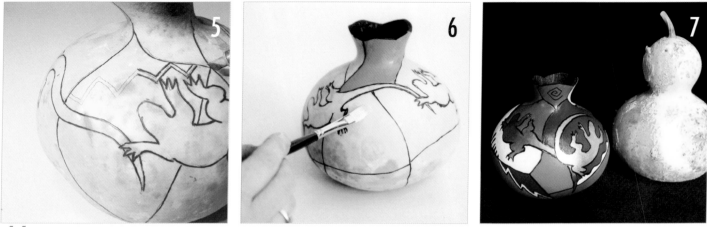

HOLDING THE PAST TOGETHER

Artist

Jenni Christensen

I n many ways, it's hard to believe Jenni Christensen lives in Utah, so far from a major organ; her heart, it seems, resides in Hawaii. Or perhaps she just carries Hawaii in her heart, because it certainly shows in her work: the lush, tropical flowers of the islands.

Still nostalgic about her youth in Hawaii, Christensen now recalls artistic impulses emerging when she was just eleven. "It all started when I was in a bird-drawing contest for all the islands," from which came a lot of positive feedback. This evolved into creating scenery for high school productions and expanding artistic horizons.

By the time Christensen finished high school, the family had moved to Idaho, a decidedly un-tropical environment. Would native flowers have been her focus had she not left Hawaii? Hard to know. But the move did direct Christensen toward Brigham Young University, where she earned a degree in fine arts and an MFA in printmaking.

A home practically filled with tropical floral prints demonstrates that Christensen's stock-in-trade has been and is printmaking. Still, five or six years ago she became curious about working with a three-dimensional canvas. Since then, gourds have gradually worked their way into her portfolio and are now "about one-third of what I do."

Important to Christensen is working with gourds in their natural state. Give her pieces a shake and you can hear seeds rattle inside. "I don't cut them," she explains. "I like the fact they're more sculptural when they're whole, when they're not decapitated."

Christensen's luminous prints hang in U.S. embassies in Lagos and Manila, so it is unsurprising that her gourds are also receiving recognition. In 2004, they were featured at Salt Lake's Rose Wagner Performing Arts Center, and pieces are also kept at the fine-arts museum at Brigham Young and in various private collections.

MOON FLOWERS

SUN FLOWERS

ANTHURIAMS

49

Project

RED LILIES

The techniques Christensen uses on her gourds are an extension of the etching she has done for years in print-making, and they are also the result of significant trial and error. Initially, she tried several applications and embellishments before arriving at a finish that allows the natural textures and flaws of the gourd to show through. While not technically difficult, the gourd created here is aesthetically rather challenging in that the creator needs to create freehand natural-looking flora and coordinate the space on the gourd.

MATERIALS
- Gourd
- Liquin
- Mineral oil
- Oil paints: black, greens, oranges, reds
- Powdered pigment: dark
- Spray varnish: clear, glossy or satin finish

TOOLS
- Eraser
- Etching needle
- Foam brush
- Mechanical pencil
- Paintbrushes

STEP ONE: Clean the outside of the gourd (see page 9). The size and shape of the gourd don't necessarily have any bearing on the nature of this project, but for this piece Christensen chooses a gourd roughly 8" tall and 15" across. She doesn't sand the gourd, even lightly, before beginning work on it.

STEP TWO: Draw the design on the gourd. This is an admittedly abstract and subjective step, so the artist must not get easily discouraged or work without something handy with which to erase (see photo 1). In creating the design, Christensen aims for a "three-dimensional painting" appearance, and is ever conscious of both negative and positive space in what she is drawing.

Tip: Christensen's familiarity with flowers and her artistic background are obviously very helpful with this piece. Similarly helpful to aspiring artists might be a book of tropical flora as one tries to re-create complex stamens, pistils, stems and leaves.

STEP THREE: Etch the pattern into the surface of the gourd. Christensen adopted this technique to give the finished piece depth and detail. Using the etching needle and holding the gourd in her lap, she simply follows the pencil lines from her sketch and creates shallow, coordinated furrows all over the gourd (see photo 2).

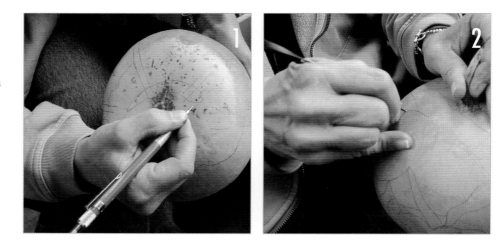

STEP FOUR: Notice that after the gourd has been etched, it still has a somewhat two-dimensional appearance. To counter that, Christensen uses an African technique in mixing dark powdered pigment with mineral oil in a ratio of roughly 1:3. She then uses a simple foam brush to apply the mixture, making sure it gets into the etched areas well (see photo 3). After wiping the pigment and oil mixture off, notice that the etched lines are darker, stand out more, and lend depth to the piece (see photo 4).

Note: As is evident in photo 4, the pigment and oil mixture can be applied before or after paint. In this example, Christensen began working on part of the color combination for this piece before moving to the pigment and oil application. Whichever comes first is up to the artist.

STEP FIVE: Paint the negative space on the gourd with oil paints. Clearly identify the negative space as separate from the positive and fill that in with a dark oil paint. Exactly what dark color to use is up to the artist; sometimes Christensen will use black, sometimes dark blue. However, she always combines her paints with an agent called liquin, which thins the paint and speeds the drying time. With both liquin and a dab of each oil paint on a palette, she simply mixes a bit of both on a brush and applies the mixture. With the negative space filled, it is possible to clearly identify where the various plants and flowers begin and end.

STEP SIX: Apply color to the positive space. For this piece, Christensen uses a mixture of reds and greens, with orange for the central portions of the flowers. Far from having a standard repertoire, she says the colors used on each piece are fairly arbitrary. She often goes over an area two or three times to get the effect she wants (see photo 5). Of course, liquin is utilized with the paints for the positive space as well.

Note: Crucial to Christensen's finished pieces (see photo gallery) are varied and layered hues of the same colors. The upper petals of a flower may be a fairly vibrant yellow, while those beneath are a bit darker, or are mottled, or receive a bit of shade; the leaves and other flora often appear as various shades of green or brown.

STEP SEVEN: Protect the finished piece. Christensen uses a spray on clear varnish in satin or glossy finish, and applies as many coats as seem necessary. If, after the first coat dries, coverage of the piece does not seem uniform, spray on another, and put extra coats on the bottom of the gourd to protect against scratching.

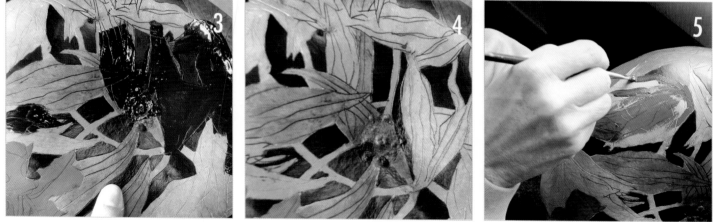

51

Lisa Conner

Having an obsessive personality is not necessarily a bad thing, right? You're thinking, "It really depends on the obsession." Exactly right. Like so many people in Northern California, Lisa Conner was, not long ago, obsessed with her work and career. Originally from Sunnyvale, she did what everyone does to survive in that place. "I worked long hours," she explains quite simply and accurately. However, while living the Northern California lifestyle, Conner also managed to find time approximately three years ago for a class in gourd arts, after which everything began to change. Now, not only was it frustrating to work so much, but she also had to deal with the tiny apartments and no work space, which effectively put gourding on hold.

So she packed it in, moved to the Land of Enchantment, and found a new obsession. "Since I arrived in New Mexico and attended my first open studio featuring other local gourd artists, it's all I can think about," Conner says. "I dream about gourds all night and work on them all day. My husband says I'm obsessed." What an observative guy! "Just because all I do is think about gourds," she says with a grin, "but obsessed? I'm not the obsessive type. Yeah, right!"

Upon moving to Rio Rancho, a verdant belt of flora along the Rio Grande, her first challenge was finding someone with whom to share her obsession. Finally, she came upon the New Mexico Gourd Society, a local chapter of the American Gourd Society. "The NMGS is a group of local gourd artists who, like myself, share a love and a healthy obsession for gourd art," she says. "I look forward to a long and healthy passion/obsession for gourds in the future." Thank God. Being obsessed can be such a lonely experience.

Remarkable as it may seem, having viewed her work, Conner is still a relative novice at gourd arts compared with some of her peers. In keeping with her personality, she makes up for a lack of experience with a wealth of energy. "I just dove in and learned as much about technique and style as I possibly could," she explains. "Trial and error. I've taken a few basic classes, and then just tried other techniques on my own."

BLUE KOKOPELLI

CIRCLES

LEAF RING

IN JUDY DORMANDY'S COLLECTION

53

Project

TAIL CHASER

Look as close as you want, but you won't see a hint of Northern California in this finished piece. Regardless of where she was raised, Conner says she has always been drawn artistically to the Southwest and Native American designs. So Tail Chaser can be attributed to her move southward, or it could be that she just had these tendencies in her the whole time. The right obsession simply brought them to the surface.

MATERIALS
• Acrylic paint: black
• Cabochons: turquoise
• Epoxy
• Gourd
• Leather dye: mahogany
• Spray acrylic sealer: satin finish

TOOLS
• Foam brush or white cotton cloth for leather dye
• Hard-lead mechanical pencil
• Heavy paper or tracing paper for lizard template
• Mini jigsaw
• Paintbrush: small
• Sandpapers: coarse, fine, medium grits
• Utility knife or awl
• Wood-burning tool with fine (5-A) tip

STEP ONE: Clean the outside of the gourd (see page 9). For this piece, Conner uses a gourd roughly 9" in diameter and 6"–7" tall. She then marks off a fairly large area around the stem and cuts it out using a mini jigsaw (see photo 5). Finally, she cleans the pulp and seeds out of the open gourd and sands the interior with coarse-grit sandpaper. Sand the edge of the gourd as well, only more lightly and with medium-grit sandpaper.

Note: In photos of the finished piece, it is possible to see that instead of making a round cut on top of the gourd, Conner removes a tear-shaped piece for a more decorative finish. Of course, this choice is up to the individual artist.

STEP TWO: Draw the lizard pattern on the outside of the gourd. First, either freehand or based on an existing design, create a lizard pattern on a piece of paper (see photo 1). When satisfied with the result, cut the template out and trace it onto the top third of the gourd, reversing the template back and forth and going around the gourd until the lizards meet. Be prepared to erase a few lizards, if necessary.

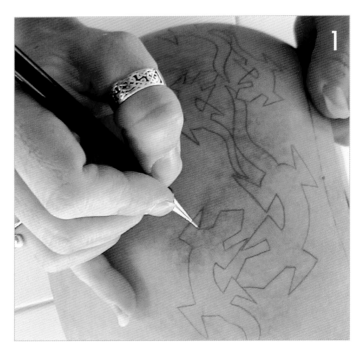

Tip: Don't try to arrange the lizards in a horizontal line. It will be difficult to make them match up this way, and it won't necessarily create an appealing piece.

STEP THREE: Burn the lizard design into the gourd surface. Using a wood-burning tool with a fine tip, burn both the lizards and the decorative rim of the gourd (see photo 2), which "should be about an inch or so below the opening," Conner says.

STEP FOUR: Cut out some, but not all of the lizards. Using a utility knife or awl, make a hole in each of the lizards intended for removal—Conner removes four lizards intermittently from the gourd. Use the mini jigsaw and, starting with the hole in each lizard (see photo 3), carefully cut along the lines burned around each one. Using fine-grit sandpaper, gently sand the insides of each cut lizard area.

STEP FIVE: Dye the entire gourd. Using a mahogany leather dye and small foam brush or a clean cotton cloth, Conner simply brushes dye on the entire gourd, starting with the inside and working out. Let dry for at least half an hour.

STEP SIX: Paint the lizards black. Using black acrylic paint and a small brush, paint all of the lizards black that were not cut out (see photo 4), making certain to also carefully paint the inside of each cut area. Paint the rim black, taking care not to paint the inside edge. Let the paint dry for about an hour.

STEP SEVEN: Protect the finished piece by spraying on a light coat of satin sealer. Apply two or three coats, letting each one dry before applying the next.

STEP EIGHT: Embellish the painted lizards. After the sealer is dry, use an epoxy or superglue to adhere one turquoise cabochon to the back of some of the painted lizards (see photo 5). Now, put the gourd where all friends and acquaintances can see it!

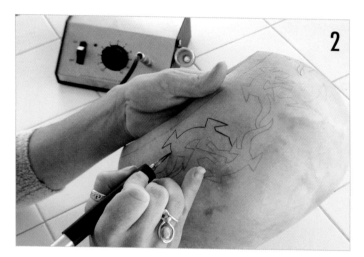

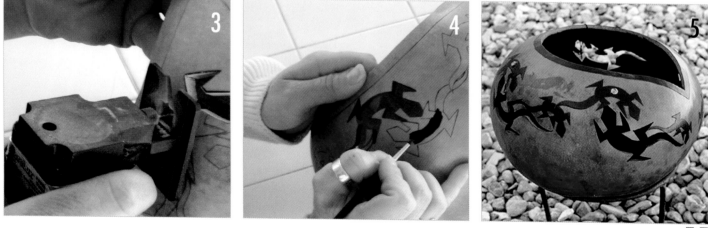

Artist

Emily Dillard

For Emily Dillard, a passion for gourds and enthusiasm for travel mean she always has someplace to go. Just try the experiment. Put "Emily Dillard" and "gourds" into Google and see the results. There she is winning a ribbon for wearable gourd art in North Carolina. She's teaching a class at the Kentucky Gourd Show, as well as the Florida Gourd Society's 2005 show. We know she was at Gourd Fest in 2002, and a show in San Diego in 2003, where she taught a class. This Emily Dillard really gets around.

"My husband and I enjoy traveling to all parts of the country to visit galleries and attend gourd shows," Dillard explains casually. So which came first, the travel or the gourds? The interest in gourds began with a visit to an arts-and-crafts festival in Kentucky, she explains, so travel seems to win the chicken-and-egg award.

In truth, gourds were just the most recent manifestation of Dillard's lifelong interest in artistic pursuits. She started drawing at age five, took painting lessons in high school, enrolled in art classes at Indiana University, and later added an endorsement in art to her teaching license. The discovery of gourds coincided with her retirement from the Indianapolis Public Schools system, where she was an ESL teacher in the Adult Division.

From the use of wood-burning and acrylic paints, Dillard has progressed through gourd sculpture, and colored pencils and inks. "There is simply no end to the things that can be done with gourds," she says. "For that, I am very grateful." Currently, Dillard is inspired by decoupage, working in it almost exclusively. To that she adds techniques like microwave pressed flowers and foliage, as well as original ink drawings.

Dillard has shown her work in the Fallbrook, California, Art and Cultural Center and the Eiteljorg Museum in Indianapolis, and has participated in the Studio Showcase and In the Works shows near her home in Zionsville, Indiana. At the North Carolina festival mentioned previously, Dillard won Best in Show for the advanced division, and has numerous additional ribbons and awards to her credit.

FALLBROOK

ROSE BOWL

DRAPED IN GOLD

57

Project

GILDED LEAVES ON A GOURD

There are two reasons I enjoy using this technique when working with gourds," Dillard says. "First, it produces excellent texture and a three-dimensional effect; and second, it gives me a chance to use some gourds whose shape is great, but whose surface leaves a lot to be desired." The gourd used in the creation of this piece, for example, is a bit oddly shaped and has been chewed by rodents. Thus, it is an excellent example of how Dillard's techniques can be utilized to enhance a gourd regardless of its condition.

MATERIALS

• Acrylic primer: dark olive green
• Decoupage mediums: regular, semigloss finishes
• Dried leaves
• Fabric paint (squeeze bottle): orange
• Gesso: black
• Gilder's pastes: copper, antique gold
• Gourd
• Metallic wax (tube variety): gold leaf
• Permanent ink pen: gold

TOOLS

• Masking tape
• Mini jigsaw
• Paintbrushes: large
• Pencil
• Sandpaper: fine grit

STEP ONE: After choosing a gourd, Dillard decides where she wants to cut off the top, then makes a level cut with a mini jigsaw. Notice that she adds an extra design element by cutting a decorative notch on one side of the gourd (see photo 1). She then cleans both the inside and outside of the gourd (see pages 9–11), and also lightly sands the rim.

STEP TWO: Paint the inside of the gourd. Dillard chooses black gesso (a thick acrylic paint) for the inside of the gourd, and brushes it on with a brush long enough to reach the bottom of the gourd and get all sides. Now the gourd is ready to be embellished!

STEP THREE: Select leaves for the decoupage surface of the gourd. "After choosing the gourd, I delve into my vast collection of dried, pressed leaves," Dillard says. "Although I also decoupage flowers onto gourds, this particular technique only works with dried leaves." She uses a microwave flower press to dehydrate leaves, but says that conventionally dried leaves will work just as well for this project.

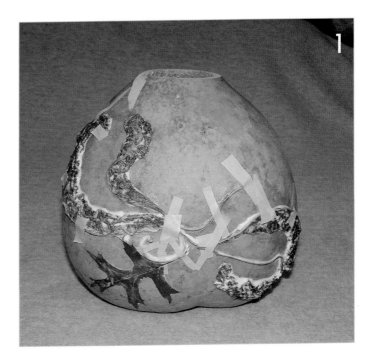

STEP FOUR: Apply leaves to the surface of the gourd. How this is done is the artist's discretion, but of course some sort of decorative arrangement is preferable (see photo 1). Brush the decoupage medium onto the backs of the leaves, attach them to the gourd, then brush more gel over the leaves, sealing them with backstrokes of the brush. Dillard uses small pieces of masking tape where necessary to hold stems and leaves until they dry completely, usually overnight.

STEP FIVE: Paint an acrylic base coat on the entire piece. For this, Dillard chooses an olive green color and paints over everything (see photo 2). Remember to remove the masking tape before applying the base coat. Let the acrylic dry at least an hour. "Choose a base color that will go with your surface color well," she advises.

STEP SIX: Using fingers, rub waxes onto the decoupaged surface of the gourd. Dillard first uses metallic copper and antique gold gilder's pastes and simply rubs the two compounds together over the leaves "in a circular pattern, blending the two colors together as I go. I also go over the entire gourd with a lighter touch" (see photo 3). She then uses a second metallic wax in gold leafing and goes over the raised areas of the gourd (the leaves, primarily) to create sort of a metallic relief against the gourd background. Avoid getting big globs of wax mixture on the gourd as it is hard to remove when dry.

Note: Dillard says: "By blending the wax colors over the part of the gourd that was rodent-eaten, I have not only sealed the unprotected inner shell, but I have also created an interesting textural area."

STEP SEVEN: Add finishing details to the piece. Dillard places bright orange "berries" on some of the leaves, using dots of fabric paint; she then outlines some of the leaves, using a gold permanent ink pen, and uses the same pen to color the rim (see photo 4).

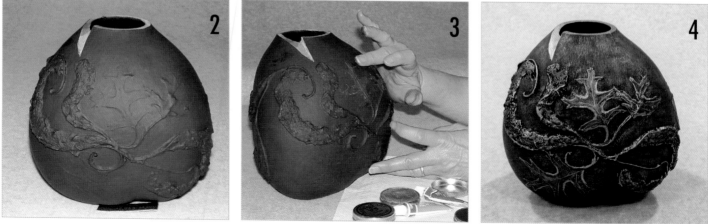

Artist

Deborah Easley

The man most certainly did not say "gourds for gourd's sake." But with regard to Deborah Easley's work, he may as well have. What French philosopher Benjamin Constant did say in 1804 was that society must have "art for art's sake, with no purpose, for any purpose perverts art. But art achieves a purpose which is not its own." For Easley, that purpose is beauty, but not necessarily through the augmentation of gourds. "I live with many raw gourds, which remain untouched—they are perfection in and of themselves."

In espousing such a philosophy, Easley is fully cognizant of the responsibility for utilizing gourds in a way that enhances their being and nature. "Any added embellishment must bring out more of the gourd's intrinsic nature, or it fails as art," she explains. "The space between the designs is equally, if not more important than the design or pattern imposed on it. Gourd art stands on its own."

So if design works to serve and enhance the natural gourd, casual or hasty approaches to enhancement miss the mark. Naturally, the process of gourd art is extended and becomes more complex, but not superfluously so. "Making gourd art hasn't gotten any easier," Easley says. "There are too many things to consider—if you make a mistake, it's difficult to undo, but if you go with the mistake, go with this entirely new flow, pieces take on a life of their own."

Each piece is a new challenge, an awakening, a fresh perspective. Many, if not all, gourd artists are energized by the uniqueness of each gourd; but Easley's perspective on this individuality is slightly different in that she asks that the gourd be a higher ideal than the art. "I'm not trying to make an artistic statement with gourd art; my goal is to take the natural beauty found in gourds and take it to another dynamic level, if that's possible, through creativity and originality. That is my challenge."

A 1996 graduate of the California School of Professional Fabric Design, Easley now calls rural Colorado home. Her work has received awards from the California Gourd Society, and has been recognized in a number of magazines dedicated to gourds and crafts in general. Before turning to gourds, she painted in gouache and watercolors (still sometimes used on gourds), and is currently studying Tibetan thangka painting.

RED

DOUBLE

PAINTED POT

PYTHON

61

Project

KIMONO

The obvious inspiration for this piece is a Japanese kimono. In an effort to make Kimono appear masculine and coordinate with the design of the glass medallion on the chest, Easley uses a subdued color palette. In looking over the steps and processes in this piece, Easley encourages the creator to "be individual and create! Use different colors, different designs, different neck openings and embellishments. Incorporate unexpected results and accidents!"

MATERIALS

- Acrylic paints or leather paints: navy blue, yellow ochre or yellow oxide
- Acrylic wood sealer: white
- Gourd
- Medallion (Easley uses dichroic glass)
- Mosaic adhesive or industrial-strength glue gel (must dry clear)
- Spray glaze: thick clear
- Tile grout: mosaic or regular

TOOLS

- Bamboo skewer
- Cotton swabs
- Flexible ruler
- Gourd scraper
- Hand gouge or routing tool
- Isopropyl alcohol
- Masking tape
- Mini jigsaw
- Paintbrushes: long-handled stiff brush, soft round watercolor brush with fine tip
- Paper towels
- Pencil
- Photocopier
- Sandpapers: 100–120-grit, 220-grit wet
- Scissors
- Transfer paper (unwaxed) or wood-burning tool with transfer tip
- Utility knife

STEP ONE: Clean the outside of the gourd (see page 9). Easley uses a gourd about 12" tall with a flat base, and warns against scratching the gourd surface in cleaning as much of the natural color and finish is evident in the final piece.

STEP TWO: Lightly sand the surface of the gourd. Wet both the gourd and a piece of 220-grit sandpaper, then sand the gourd just until smooth. Avoid sanding too deeply and revealing the "quick" of the gourd—the white underlayer just beneath the brownish surface. Rinse the gourd and pat it dry.

STEP THREE: Sketch the neckline of the Kimono on the gourd. Easley recommends looking over the gourd and determining which part should be the front, then simply using a pencil to draw the neckline in preparation for cutting. Mistakes (and there will be some!) can be removed with a cotton swab and a bit of alcohol.

STEP FOUR: Cut along the lines drawn for the neckline (see photo 1). A sturdy utility knife should work to make the cuts as long as the gourd is not too thick. Otherwise, use a mini jigsaw, starting with a small incision made with the utility knife in the area that will be cut away.

STEP FIVE: Clean the inside of the gourd with a gourd scraper and discard the interior seeds and other material (see page 11). Sand the inside of the gourd and the neckline with moderate grade (100–200 grit) sandpaper. Since the interior of the gourd will be fairly evident upon completion, Easley recommends sanding the interior "as smooth and flat as possible." Rinse out the inside repeatedly and pat dry.

STEP SIX: Create a notch for the medallion. First, either hold the medallion in place or tape it to the gourd just below where the neckline comes to a point. Trace around the medallion with a pencil and remove it. Using either a small hand gouge or a routing tool, carve out the circular area for the medallion, taking care not to go completely through the gourd (see photo 1). "Your goal is to be able to place the medallion into the recessed area so that it lays flat against the gourd with as little room as possible between the edge of the medallion and the edge of the recessed area," Easley says. Use a small piece of 100–120-grit sandpaper to lightly smooth out the interior and edges of the recessed area. Wipe clean with a wet paper towel.

Tip: In the previous step, one of Easley's concerns when working with a small hand gouge is that the tool will slip and mark up the exterior of the gourd. "Hold your hand gouge firmly," she cautions, making certain you have a stable grip on the tool.

STEP SEVEN: In pencil, draw the neckband around the neckline and down across the gourd to the base (see photo 1). Using a flexible ruler, Easley makes regularly and fairly closely spaced pencil marks roughly ³/₄" from the neck opening and then connects the marks by hand to make the lines.

STEP EIGHT: Paint the interior of the gourd. Using a stiff long-handled brush, paint the entire inside of the gourd and the carved notch with white wood sealer or primer. If unpainted spots remain inside the gourd, Easley recommends pouring a bit of paint inside the gourd and swirling

it around, then pouring the excess out "being careful not to drip on the exterior of the gourd." If dripping occurs, wipe with a wet paper towel. Let the interior dry completely.

STEP NINE: Using either yellow oxide acrylic paint or yellow ochre, paint the interior of the gourd again, following the same procedure as in Step Eight. Paint the carved notch with the same color (see photo 2). If the first coat does not adequately cover the primer coat both inside the gourd and in the carved area, add another after the first coat is dry.

STEP TEN: Paint the neckband of the Kimono. Using either acrylic paint or leather paint in navy blue, carefully color the neckband using the pointed tip of a small, round watercolor brush to create clean edges. "Remember," Easley advises, "two thin coats are better than one thick one." Make sure to paint the sanded rim of the gourd as well.

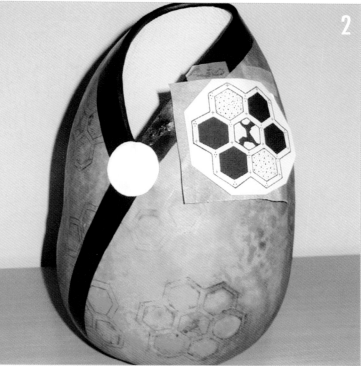

STEP ELEVEN: Transfer the hexagonal Pattern A onto the gourd exterior (see photo 3). Photocopy the pattern first; reduce or enlarge it as desired. Tape it to the gourd over unwaxed transfer paper and trace the lines with a pencil (see photo 2 on page 63). Trace only the lines of the pattern, adding dots and filled areas later with paint. An alternative transfer method is to use the hot tool's transfer tip. Easley recommends both "scattering" the patterns and "connecting them in places. Be creative with the placement." Also, leave space for the gourd skin to show through, and use just one or two hexagons from the overall design to fill in some spaces.

Note: Easley coordinates the pattern at the center of the hexagonal design with the pattern in the medallion, and advises others to "use any substitution that works for your centerpiece."

STEP TWELVE: Paint the patterns on the gourd's surface. Using the round watercolor brush, paint the hexagonal patterns as shown in photo three. First, fill in each pattern using the yellow oxide or yellow ochre acrylic (see photo 3). When the yellow has dried completely, apply navy blue outlines and fill-ins. Use the edge of the brush for outlining. Hold the tip of the brush perpendicular to the gourd to make the small dots. Let the paint dry completely.

STEP THIRTEEN: Apply two light coats of thick clear glaze, allowing the gourd to dry between each coat. Let the finished piece dry for twenty-four hours after the final coat.

STEP FOURTEEN: Insert and grout the medallion. Apply tile adhesive or industrial-strength glue to the back of the medallion and insert it into the carved circular area. Let this cure for five or six hours before carefully applying grout to the crevices between the medallion and the edge of the recessed area. "I use a sharp-tipped bamboo skewer with tiny bits of grout and gently poke it into the gaps," Easley says. Keep filling until any gaps are smooth and level with the gourd, then let the grout dry for approximately half an hour. When the grout is set, wipe off any excess with a wet paper towel, being careful not to smear the painted areas.

Tip: Whether or not to paint the grout is up to the artist. Easley chooses to apply a bit of navy blue leather paint to the grout when it is completely dry and set.

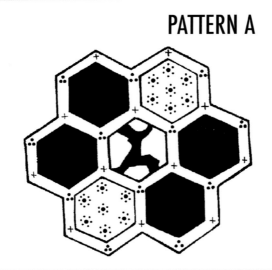

PATTERN A

3

KIMONO

Artist

Bonnie Gibson

While Bonnie Gibson doesn't object to being called a "hobby junky" (her term), she would prefer "artisan" or "craftsman" in reference to the creation of her finished gourd pieces. Reportedly, Michelangelo also lifted an eyebrow whenever the Italian media referred to him as "marble freak" instead of "sculptor."

Gibson has earned the more refined designation. A self-taught artist, she has pursued creative endeavors for more than thirty years, and her Arizona home is filled with prize-winning efforts in scale miniatures, scrimshaw, woodcarving, lost-wax casting, glass etching/fusing, and (banal-sounding by comparison) painting and sculpture.

As Gibson sees it now, "it was inevitable that I would eventually be drawn to the humble gourd as a versatile and challenging canvas." The years of experience with other media enable Gibson to apply borrowed techniques to gourd art. "Some gourds are inlaid with carved eggshell, glass or gemstones; others are deeply carved in highly dimensional sculpted relief, and most reflect my deep interest in the native cultures of the Southwest."

While many artists see gourds as a three-dimensional canvas, Gibson goes the extra step of adding another dimension to the surface of the gourd. Each piece is blessed with a theme, and all sides adhere to that theme in different ways; turning the gourd is like observing a highly artistic and visually impressive slide show.

"I am always searching for innovative new materials or techniques that will enhance my work," Gibson explains. These explorations have enabled her to perfect techniques and effects such as carved sand ripples and faux basketry, gold leafing and patina-oxidized paints, and various types of inlay.

In addition to working on individual gourd art pieces, Gibson keeps a very active schedule in attending festivals and shows, teaching others what she has learned about gourd art, and writing her own how-to books on the subject.

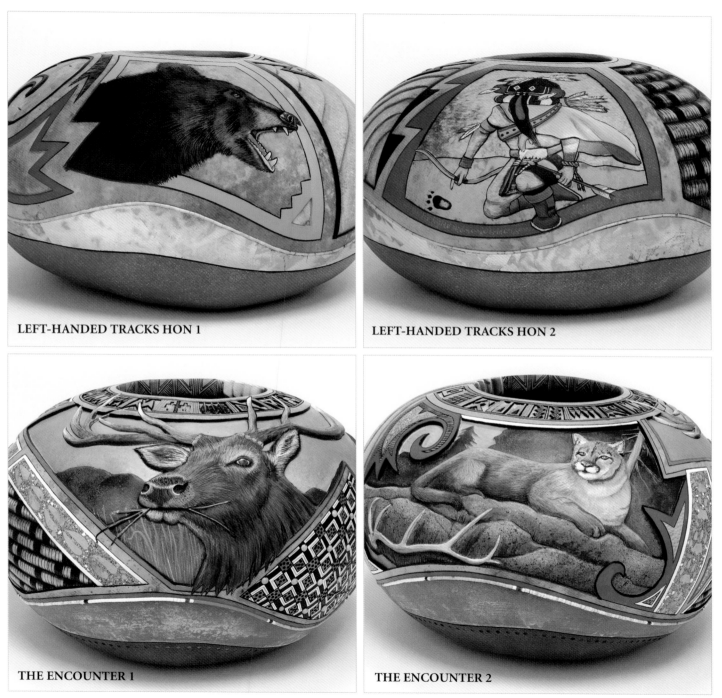

LEFT-HANDED TRACKS HON 1

LEFT-HANDED TRACKS HON 2

THE ENCOUNTER 1

THE ENCOUNTER 2

67

Project

DESERT RAM

This particular piece is an excellent example of Gibson's style. As is often the case, she chose an initial theme, this one being a Desert Big Horn Sheep. Notice in particular some of the signature items on Desert Ram indicative of Gibson's work: the carved sand ripples, the patina-oxidized paint, inlaid stone, and faux rock art and ancient cultural paintings.

MATERIALS

- Acrylic paints: assorted colors including copper metallic
- Cabochons: (8) 5mm turquoise
- Gap-filling cyanoacrylate superglue
- Gourd: large canteen with thick walls
- Gourd scrap for lid
- Heishi beads: brown lip shell
- Oxidizer: blue patina
- Pine wood, scrap piece for lid
- Protective finishes: spray-on matte; brush-on gloss
- Resin inlay: turquoise
- Spray lacquer
- Wood glue

TOOLS

- Baby wipes or paper towels
- Carving tools: high-speed air-driven tool with small carbide dental bits, and high-speed steel cutters (wheel, ball, inverted cone), rotary tool with structured tooth carbide burs (flame, ball cylinder)
- Mini cross saw
- Mini disk sander
- Paintbrushes: fine liner, medium round, wide flat
- Pencil
- Permanent marker: black fine tip
- Riffler files: fine-cutting small-needle files with curved ends
- Sandpapers: fine grits
- Sea sponge
- Toothbrush
- Wood-burning tool

STEP ONE: Clean the outside of the gourd. Let the gourd dry completely (see page 9). For the Desert Ram, Gibson selects a gourd roughly 16" in diameter with thick walls; thickness is very important when approaching the carving process. Look over it carefully and determine the theme and design elements of the final piece. What should the final piece look like? What theme would carry the entire piece? What is the artistic vision?

STEP TWO: Sketch the design onto the surface of the gourd. Of course, much of this process is trial and error, and Gibson says moist baby wipes or damp paper towels will come in very handy for removing undesired elements (see photo 1). In creating her design, Gibson usually pays only passing attention to the bottom of the gourd. "I often design the bottom third of the gourd with a simple decorative wave-like feature," she explains, permitting more time for the upper two-thirds.

Note: This early design process is neither easy nor quick, but is key in effectively determining the final outcome of the project. Gibson visualizes all aspects of Desert Ram in this early stage. "I usually plan for two or three main focal points, several smaller accenting areas, and decorative borders to unify the overall design. This gourd has several large design elements; a close up portrait of a ram head, a night scene with a ram standing on a precipice, and a Hopi ram katsina figure. Other areas are filled with smaller designs such as faux basketry, and some use designs that further develop the ram theme, such as ram petroglyphs and pottery shards" (see photos for examples).

STEP THREE: When satisfied with the overall design, go over the penciled lines with a fine-point permanent marker. This prevents smudging and blurring during later stages. Wipe off lingering pencil marks. Gibson also determines at this point whether or not the final piece will have a lid, as Desert Ram does. A lid, she explains, "can add a dramatic accent and increase the effectiveness of the overall design," but it is time consuming.

STEP FOUR: Choose a panel to begin carving. Where one starts is entirely the discretion of the artist and the level of comfort one feels with the tools. For the purpose of these instructions, starting with a relatively straightforward panel such as the carved sand ripples is advised. Using a rotary tool and an inverted cone-shaped bur, begin slowly to structure the sand ripples. Start by carving lines where the bottoms of the ripples will fall, then gradually structure waves from one ripple to the next (see photo 2). Be careful not to go too deep and puncture the gourd.

Note: Clearly, which tools to use are important to the carving process, particularly burs and bits. Experimenting on gourd scraps before use is a good idea, and Gibson says the choice of exactly which burs and bits to use "depend a lot on an individual's preferences." She prefers structured-tooth carbide burs, which are "covered in tiny needle-like projections to cut cleanly and quickly without clogging." Most often, Gibson uses wheel, ball and inverted cone-shaped bits.

STEP FIVE: Continue carving other panels. The emergence of the ram and Hopi figures will come through relief carving: removing material around a subject until it is raised against a flat background (see photo 3, 5–7). Again, Gibson cautions against misjudging depth and "piercing the gourd shell." Add greater depth to the subjects by rounding the edges at varying depths and carving details to make the subject more lifelike, real, and tangible. Light carving for a rock-like appearance gives the petroglyph panel it's unique look.

Tip: For final detail carving and texturing, Gibson uses an air-driven high-speed tool similar to a dental drill. This tool runs approximately ten times faster than a regular rotary tool, and employs small dental burs for quick, precise cutting. If such a tool is not available, similar effects can be created using a wood-burning tool with a fine tip. "The burning tool can be used to simulate textures such as fur or feathers, and it is also a great tool for adding decorative patterns to the borders and other areas that are not decorated with carving."

2

STEP SIX: Carve out recessed border areas that will receive inlayed stones or stone resin (see photo 3). Where the ram and the Hopi figure are brought to life by rounding the edges of the subject, carving in the areas that will receive inlay should "create neat, sharp edges" waiting to be filled.

STEP SEVEN: Fill the carved border areas with faux-turquoise resin inlay. While beads and stones should not be placed until painting is complete, resin inlay is applied before painting. Gibson mixes the resin according to manufacturer's directions, fills the ram's hooves border area and a couple of recessed hoof carvings near the lid, and lets the resin dry overnight.

STEP EIGHT: Sand the resin down until it is level with the surface of the gourd. A small disk or drum sander quickly removes most of the excess resin; a final hand-sanding with fine sandpaper works well to remove the last little bit of resin, smooth out the area and remove from the resin small grooves and scratches (see photo 3). "The smoothed resin can be polished to bring out a shiny finish," Gibson says, "or it can be coated with a thin layer of brushed on gloss sealer."

STEP NINE: Using progressively finer grits of sandpaper, smooth down lingering rough areas all over the gourd. Work carefully, making certain not to oversand and remove carved details, while still smoothing out carved areas. For areas sandpaper can't get to, Gibson recommends using small riffler files.

STEP TEN: Lightly apply a lacquer spray to the carved areas. Gibson recommends just a "light mist" of the spray to seal the "meat" in the carved areas and prevent "swelling or lifting of gourd fibers" during the painting. Wipe off excess from the uncarved areas before painting.

STEP ELEVEN: Give the carved marvel a colorful finish! Start with the bottom of the gourd beneath the "wave" border. Gibson paints this area with a copper metallic surfacing paint, then coats the area with a blue patina oxidizer while the paint is still damp to create interesting effects (see photo 5). Let the area dry completely.

STEP TWELVE: Paint the rest of the gourd. Gibson uses acrylic paints in a variety and number of colors determined by the subject matter. She prefers to complete one section or panel before moving to the next. The panel with the Hopi figure is a good example of the techniques she uses on the entire piece (see photo 6). Notice the intricate painted details on clothing, the headdress and the staff. She also applies sponged white clouds to the background in both the Hopi panel and the close-up of the ram's head (see photo 4). In the panel of the ram standing on rocks (see photo 5), create stars by dipping an old toothbrush in paint and rubbing a finger across the bristles to spatter the paint. Next to that panel, paint a faux hole in a broken pottery shard.

Tip: A few different brushes will be needed to paint Desert Ram or similar pieces (see tools list). Narrow brushes with fine, rounded tips will be very useful in applying intricate details. To avoid brush marks, Gibson applies several thin coats of paint instead of one thick one. For billowy white clouds, she uses a small sea sponge that is dipped in paint, blotted on a piece of paper, then lightly dabbed on areas of the gourd. A common color—dark red, in this case—is used on all borders to unify the piece.

STEP THIRTEEN: Spray the finished gourd with one or two coats of matte sealer, allowing it to dry between coats. Gibson likes to also brush a glossy finish over the ram's eyes to bring it to life, plus a bit on the inlay resin for luster and sheen.

STEP FOURTEEN: Glue cabochons, beads, glass, or other embellishments to the surface of the piece. On Desert Ram, Gibson glues smallish turquoise stones around the rim near the lid, using the gap-filling glue. This type of glue, she explains, is thicker than usual superglue and will sit on the surface of the gourd for a bit. This allows a bit of cushion in applying the stones, but provides a strong bond when cured. At this point, she also glues the brown heishi beads into the inlay groove separating the panels from the oxidized bottom area.

Artist

Geri Wood-Gittings

Geri Wood-Gittings began responding to creative impulses before she could drive, and was winning awards before she could vote. She was asked to create ads and company logos before she even finished high school. By definition, Gittings's artistic devotion is referred to as a calling, and society demonstrates that such phenomena are relatively rare.

Raised in Wausau, Wisconsin, and completely self-taught, Gittings "started drawing figures, various animals and scenery as soon as I was old enough to hold a pencil. I drew and painted portraits of my family and friends whenever I could get them to sit long enough." And she kept those initial attempts to track her own progress.

School was just another place for Gittings to practice her craft. "I got disciplined more times than not for drawing," she recalls now. But that education did have a practical reward. After graduation, a teacher who Gittings had drawn recommended her to the art director at Wausau Insurance, providing the payoff for uninterrupted artistic pursuit.

Gittings later married Bob Wood, himself a talented artist who suggested they move to Kalispell, Montana, to "starve together painting the West." For Gittings, the time spent in Montana was not without reward as she was and is still featured in the permanent collections of the Hockaday Museum of Western Art, the Pacific Northwest Indian Center, the Leanin' Tree Museum of Western Art, and many private collections.

Currently living in Phoenix, Arizona, Gittings devotes herself full time to Southwestern art. These days, that means working on gourds. For her, gourds are simply ideal for use in exploring multiple artistic mediums. "I was born to be an artist," she explains. "That's all I was ever interested in doing." She still has the drawings from third grade to prove it.

STAR POWER

FUSED GLASS

CARVED KACHINA

73

CARVED KACHINA

This piece is an excellent example of Gittings's desire to both apply different mediums to a single creation and express the culture and history of her current home, the desert Southwest. The creation of this and similar pieces requires a steady hand and faith in your artistic abilities, as you will be asked to draw, burn, paint, and carve a single design.

MATERIALS

- Clear satin lacquer, or acrylic semigloss or gloss spray finish
- Gourd
- Leather dyes: light honey brown, green, dark red, tan, turquoise, off-white

TOOLS

- Foam brushes for dyes: $1/4"–1/2"$
- Latex glove
- Mechanical pencil
- Mild soap and water
- Paintbrush: small detail
- Rotary tool with two round engraving bits: $1/32"$ or 0.8mm for kachina detail; $3/32"$ or 2.4mm for area around kachina
- Small pillow
- Wood-burning tool with straight-line tip

STEP ONE: Clean the outside of the gourd (see page 9). For the Carved Kachina, Gittings selects a tall gourd about 5"–6" across and roughly 18"–24" tall. Check the hardness of your gourd by using the rotary tool on an area that is going to be carved. If the gourd is extremely difficult to carve,

STEP TWO: Develop an idea of the design you wish to create. It might be helpful to draw the design on paper before putting it on the gourd. The design Gittings creates here is that of a dancing kachina, a traditional doll created by Native American tribes of the Southwest. She sketches the design on the gourd in pencil (see photo 1).

STEP THREE: Burn your design into the dried gourd. When she is happy with the pencil drawing, Gittings uses her wood-burning pen to burn the kachina doll into the gourd surface (see photo 2). She recommends starting with low to medium on the tool and working up to the desired setting. Your goal, Gittings says, is to make lines that are "evenly burned and deep enough to hold the design once the dye is put on."

Tip: Gittings says that although she was "taught to pull the pen towards me while turning the gourd to follow the lines of my drawing, sometimes I do just the opposite." Do what works best at the time for you, she recommends. Also, Gittings keeps an old belt nearby to clean residue from the end of the wood-burning pen, as well as a stone and oil to keep the pen sharp.

STEP FOUR: Clean up the gourd in preparation for dyeing. You will want to eliminate any lingering pencil marks from the initial drawing, and for this Gittings recommends mild soap and water because it works better than an eraser, "plus you don't get the eraser dust."

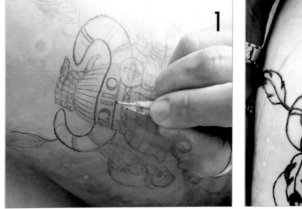

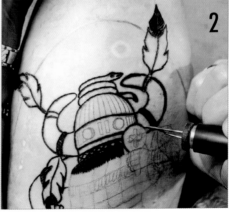

STEP FIVE: Apply leather dyes to pyrographed gourd. The areas in which Gittings is painting are small, so she insists on using a fine brush and chooses tan, dark red, turquoise, and green as a color combination (see photo 3).

Tip: The artist uses and recommends small brushes made of sable. "They are not inexpensive, but they last a long time if taken care of, and they are soft and keep their shape."

STEP SIX: Apply leather dye to the area of the gourd around the oval where the kachina is. Gittings uses a light brown to darken the substantial surface area around the kachina; this creates a view in which the kachina design and the colors really stand out on the off-white oval against a darker, honey-colored background.

STEP SEVEN: Spray the gourd with a light coat of lacquer or acrylic. Let the first coat dry and then spray the gourd again, being careful in both applications to avoid spraying so heavily the finish runs. The purpose of the spray, Gittings says, is to "protect the dye and keep it from coming off on your hands as you work on the carving."

STEP EIGHT: Prepare to carve the section of the gourd around the kachina. Gittings puts a small pillow, foam pad, or towel on her lap (something that will help hold the gourd in place) and wears a latex or leather glove on her nonworking hand for additional holding power.

STEP NINE: Start to carve, using the rotary tool and a small bit. Gittings starts by carving detail into particular aspects of the kachina itself: the feathers, headpiece, and arm, wrist, and leg bands (see photo 4). On the feathers, she carves lines following the natural curve to create texture and grain. For the headpiece, she gives the snake depth in the form of scales shaped like this: <<<<<. "Next, I carve in circles for the eyes with two thick lines in between the eyes," Gittings says. On the 'beard' hanging from the headdress, she also carves vertical lines very close together in the unburned horizontal stripes. On the arm, wrist, and leg bands, she carves curved lines to give the impression of twisted rope.

STEP TEN: Carve out the background area around the kachina and inside the wood-burned oval. Gittings recommends a large bur on the rotary tool (see photo 5). She says there is "no particular method to this other than not being exact. You just want to end up with small bumps and crevices."

STEP ELEVEN: Paint the carved area between the kachina and oval. Natural discolorations convince Gittings that she cannot just leave it alone, so she mixes and applies an acrylic paint to match the lightest portion of the carved area. When the paint is dry, apply one or two more coats of lacquer or acrylic spray (see finished piece on page 73).

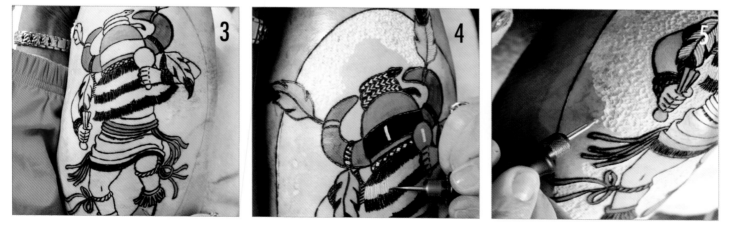

Artists

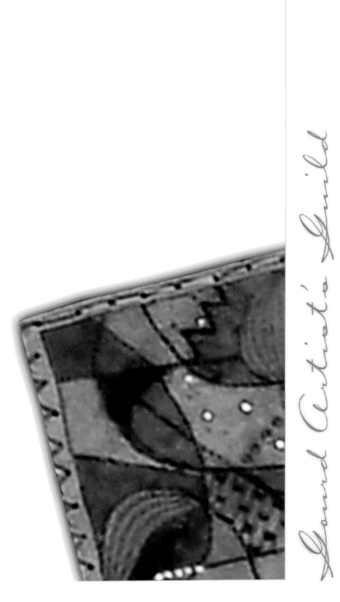

Gourd Artist's Guild

Never let is be said that gourd artists are not a close-knit, passionate and friendly group of folks. Who knew so much enthusiasm could spring up around a bitter squash?

For proof, look no further than the Gourd Patch Quilt project, an international collaborative tying together (pun absolutely intended) 112 artists from those gourding bastions of the United States, Canada and Australia. Let there be no misunderstanding, here, the Gourd Quilt is exactly what it sounds like: a quilt made from gourds. No, it does not consist of entire gourds, which would essentially make it the world's largest flotation device. Instead, the finished piece is a dazzling array of 4" x 4" gourd pieces, each completely unique, stitched together to form the top layer of a quilt.

As with so many things, the idea for the Gourd Patch Quilt started innocently enough in an online forum. Only in this case, the idea is both creative and inoffensive—even inspiring. On "Patch Pals," a section of John Stacy's Web site The Gourd Artist's Guild, people meet virtually to discuss and share a love of gourds. In May of 2003, someone suggested the quilt idea, and the clarion call went out for contributors.

The not trivial task of organization for the Gourd Patch Quilt fell to the mother/daughter team of Lynette Dawson and Margaret Schroeder. "[They] have been the threads that bind this artistic endeavor," reads information about the project. Clearly, the quilt became a labor of love for Dawson and Schroeder. As each tile arrived at their homes in Michigan, they took photos and posted them on a Web site, along with a biography of each artist.

For the contributing artists, there were no restrictions, which resulted in a finished product as diverse as it could possibly be. Pyrography, acrylic finishes, carving, inlay, paste waxes, dyes—just about every gourd arts technique is represented; but not only technique is on display. Each tile is representative also of impressive talent and vision, as well as a desire to build community and honor a shared love.

Looking through the photos of the gourd tiles is a pleasure for its eye-catching diversity and breadth of creativity. Without space to honor each tile here, it is worth a visit to the project Web site to take each of them in and read the background on the artists.

Of course, once all 112 tiles arrived in Michigan, they had to be assembled into a collective whole. Again, this task fell to Dawson and Schroeder, who for all their efforts expected nothing in the form of monetary compensation. While it may sound dramatic to describe the task undertaken in terms like "massive" and "overwhelming," statistics might better tell the whole story. Before it was finished, the quilt required six layers of material: 112 gourd tiles, one large piece of chocolate velvet automotive upholstery, 10-oz quilt batting layers, one large piece of brown cotton cloth, beige cotton quilted backing, as well as 4,807 holes, 5,168 stitches, 361.4 yards of sinew, and 396.10 yards of cotton thread. All told, the quilt itself required 465 hours to assemble; it is estimated that the entire project, with tile creation, took 1,020 hours.

"The Gourd Patch Quilt showcases the individual art styles of 112 gourd artists, uniting their beautiful styles with strong threads. These threads are symbolic of the friendships formed through the artists' creative passion for gourds.

"The center stitches represent the joining of conversations and shared techniques within the supportive community of an e-group known as The Patch Pals, sponsored by John Stacy's Gourd Artists Guild.

Todd Photographic Studio

"It's been a great honor to be entrusted with stitching together these unique quilt tiles, forming lasting bonds between gourd art and gourd friends."

Lynette Dawson and Margaret Schroeder

Project

THE GOURD PATCH QUILT

MATERIALS

- Cotton batting: (2) 10-oz. layers, at least 8' x 5'
- Cotton fabric: brown, at least 8' x 5'
- Cotton thread: dark brown
- Craft glue
- Gourd tiles: 112 4" x 4" tiles, varied designs with borders for holes
- One-ply sinew: natural color
- Velvet fabric: chocolate, at least 8' x 5'

TOOLS

- 2" x 2" lengths of wood: (2) 8' lengths; (2) 3½' lengths
- Awl
- Carpet tack strips
- Craft drill
- Hand-stitching needles: long
- Pencil
- Pliers
- Power drill
- Sandpaper: medium grit
- String
- Wood screws

STEP ONE: Post an idea on an e-mail list and then watch it spin wildly out of control on the Internet as people latch onto the idea and help generate crazy enthusiasm based on common passion.

STEP TWO: Find 112 generous and talented artists willing to donate their time and energy in making a contribution to a worthwhile project. Also identify two or more thoughtful individuals happy to coordinate the project and assemble all required materials.

STEP THREE: Construct a homemade quilt rack. For the basic frame, The Gourd Patch Quilt uses 2" x 2" pieces of wood for a rack roughly 8' x 3½'. Stabilize the rack by attaching it with wood screws to the tops of two wood sawhorses. Inside the frame attach two additional pieces of wood on each end creating a rectangular internal frame roughly 3½' x 5'—the final quilt will be 3' x 5' (see photo 1).

STEP FOUR: Place a bottom layer of brown cotton fabric over the frame, pull it as taut as possible, and secure it to the frame. Dawson and Schroeder attach carpet tack strips to the edges of the frame to hold the fabric.

STEP FIVE: Put two layers of 10-oz. cotton batting on top of the bottom fabric layer, then place a top layer over the batting. For the top layer, the Gourd Patch Quilt uses a chocolate-colored velvet fabric, which is also tacked down to the frame. Trim the batting roughly to the edge of the frame.

STEP SIX: Attach guidelines to the frame for use in arranging the tiles (see photo 1). Measure, then drill wood screws into the frame to which string will be attached to create a 3' x 5' perimeter. Also create a guideline across the center of the quilt, dividing the large rectangle into two squares.

STEP SEVEN: Arrange the tiles within the guidelines. This process requires a bit of maneuvering and patience. First, Dawson and Schroeder arrange the tiles on the velvet surface the way they like, coordinating design, color, thickness and shape (see photos 1 and 2). They also sand some of the tiles to make them fit cleanly with those adjacent. Finally, each of the tiles is numbered from 1 to 112 in case a herd of gazelle comes through and knocks the whole thing over.

STEP EIGHT: Drill holes in the tiles to attach them to the quilt. On average, there are forty-five holes drilled per gourd, for an average per side of approximately eleven holes. It is easy to see how this is a time-consuming process. Schroeder marks the tiles for drilling, after which Dawson uses an awl to make guide holes in each tile. Working together, both women use small craft drills to create holes in all the tiles (see photo 3).

STEP NINE: Glue tiles to the velvet top layer. Without adhering the tiles to the material somehow, most will shift during the stitching process. To avoid movement, Schroeder applies a bit of craft glue to the back of each. Give the glue a few hours to dry.

STEP TEN: Stitch the tiles to the quilt and do finish stitching. Dawson uses a one-ply natural sinew to attach the tiles, and dark brown cotton thread with a 5" needle to finish the quilt (see photos 4 and 5). "Basic cross stitches connect each tile," she says, "while the border is done with running stitches. Pliers are necessary to pull the needle through the quilt layers."

Artist

Barbara Holman

With art of any kind, genre is an important concept, so consider the following analogy: In a particular movie, Darth Vader engages in a pitched battle with Wyatt Earp, after which a chase ensues through the streets of New York City. Unable to catch the dark lord, Marshall Earp hires a slovenly private dick to find him, but the detective is himself done-in when one of King Arthur's knights removes his head. Make sense? Well, no, because in film, sticking with a genre is usually important for narrative success.

But what is true in film is not necessarily so with other artistic forms. In modern artistic endeavors, what Barbara Holman creates is commonly called "mixed media," the utilization of several types of media in the creation of a unified, thematic piece. So it is not at all strange that underneath her embellishments is a gourd, a fairly unique canvas in itself. "I like variety!" Holman fairly shouts. "This is the beauty of working with gourds."

Variety indeed. Holman's finished pieces are a veritable kitchen sink of media. "I use many different techniques for each art piece. These include pyrography, hand-carving, acrylics, inlay, embossing, foiling, polymer clay, powdered pigments and metallics, oil pencil, gilder's paste, copper metal and a wide variety of inks and dyes."

A self-taught artist, Holman considers her best teachers to be "time, patience, and practice." Possessed by an artistic spirit, she discovered a few years ago that this creative persona was not getting fed. In 2002, she first held a gourd in her hands. "I imagined all the cool things I could do with it! That's the moment when my gourding career began."

Born and raised in the snowy climes of Minnesota, Holman, years ago, migrated to the desert southwest and now resides in Prescott Valley, Arizona. At the heart of her creative impulses lie several influences, including Native American cultures, nature and wildlife, primitive iconology, and spirituality.

Holman's work has been featured in the Prescott, *Arizona Daily Courier,* and the May 2003 Home and Garden Expo.

MAJESTIC

FAERIE DUST & ANGEL BLESSINGS 1

FAERIE DUST & ANGEL BLESSINGS 2

MASQUERADE

81

THE ANCIENTS

"When working, I listen to both my inner voice/intuition and my heart," Holman explains. "I feel that each gourd speaks to me, revealing its own distinctive energy and vibration." If so, the energy and vibration for The Ancients are very old. Influenced by Southwestern petroglyphs, this modern version of ancient rock art is able to utilize colors and dazzle that the ancient inhabitants of the region never could have imagined.

MATERIALS

- Acrylic paints: golden bronze, iridescent bronze, burgundy, jade green, burnt orange, raw sienna, teal,
- Acrylic paints (squeeze bottles): light blue, cranberry, light green,
- Acrylic spray sealer
- Alcohol-based inks: light blue, dark brown, cranberry, terra-cotta
- Glazing medium (optional)
- Glitter: sea green, pink, fine or extra fine
- Glitter glue
- Gourd
- Lacquer, semigloss finish
- Leather dye: tan
- Metal leafing foil: variegated red
- Permanent marker: black, medium width
- Pigment powders (optional): metallic copper, brownish green
- Polyurethane spray sealer
- Size (foil adhesive)

TOOLS

- Foam brushes: 2"
- Paintbrushes: (2) small round
- Pencil
- Rag
- Rotary tool with ⅛" rounded tip
- Routing tool with #9903 tungsten carbide bit
- Sea sponge
- Stipple brush (optional)
- Tracing and transfer papers (optional)

STEP ONE: Clean the exterior of the gourd (see page 9). For The Ancients, Holman selects a gourd roughly 9" tall and 20" in circumference.

STEP TWO: Sketch the desired petroglyph/rock art design on the surface of the gourd. This is a fairly abstract process and really is the discretion of the artist. If unsure, start with sketches on paper and/or consult a book that includes examples of ancient stone art. Tracing and transfer papers are also options to consider. Notice that Holman creates "anthropomorphic" human designs, primitive animals, and enhancing details (see photo 1).

STEP THREE: Carve the outline of the sketched designs into the gourd. Using a rotary tool and a ¹/₈" bit with a rounded tip, follow the lines of the pencil sketch until the darker upper layer of the gourd is removed, revealing the white, pithy layer underneath. Holman does not carve out the interior area of the human-like or animal figures, but does add decorative elements (see photos 1 and 2).

STEP FOUR: Dye the entire gourd. Using a tan leather dye and a foam brush, apply the dye to the entire gourd, making sure it gets into all the carved crevices and crannies (see photo 3). "Wipe off any runny excess," Holman says, "and use your personal preference as to how light or dark you want it to be." For a darker finish, add more coats of dye. Let the dye dry overnight.

STEP FIVE: Apply a protective sealer to the entire gourd. Holman sprays on two coats of sealer, letting each dry before applying the next. "This will help prevent any color leakage from the dye."

STEP SIX: Sponge-paint the entire gourd. First, choose a palette of acrylic paints to apply to the gourd. Holman chooses burnt orange, jade green, burgundy, iridescent bronze, raw sienna, teal, and golden bronze; she likes to start with dark colors and move to light (see photo 4). The goal is a multicolored and mottled appearance, like a shower of confetti at Mardi Gras (see photo 5). Let the acrylic paints dry overnight.

Tip: Holman recommends using a damp sponge "for better paint coverage. Also, if you are new to the art of sponge painting, you may want to have a practice mat on which to learn how much paint to put on the sponge, how much pressure to apply, etc. I find the process easiest if I dab my sponge (paint applied) on a clean cardboard surface just prior to applying it to the gourd."

STEP SEVEN: Fill in the carved lines and designs with permanent black ink. Using a medium-width permanent marker, simply follow the carved lines and fill them in. Fill in the heads and all the design areas that are carved out.

STEP EIGHT: Add foil embellishments to the gourd. First determine what areas will be embellished with the foil and brush adhesive on those areas with a small brush. Notice that Holman uses foil to add colorful elements to designated design areas on the fronts of the human figures (see photo 6). She also uses it on the interior area of the carved petroglyph deer (not shown). Let the adhesive dry to a clear finish, then apply the foil and pull away the parts that are not adhered to the gourd. Keep the excess in a container for later use.

STEP NINE: Add splashes of color to the gourd. Using alcohol-based inks in a variety of colors, and a small, round paintbrush, select design elements and areas of the gourd to spice up with color (see photo 7). "Get creative!" Holman encourages. "Remember, this is Your project!" Photos of the finished piece show areas where she decides to apply color; the colors she chooses include cranberry, dark brown, light blue, and terra-cotta.

Allow the inks to dry for about twenty minutes. "If these inks are not available," Holman says, "substitute any of your favorite acrylics."

STEP TEN: Outline some of the carved design elements with acrylic paints. Using acrylics in small squeeze bottles, Holman lays down a bead of acrylic paint alongside carved lines thick enough to create something of a ridge, but not thick enough to run (see photo 8). Be careful with this dynamic—and wipe quickly with a wet rag if runs occur. Again, where the outlines go is the discretion of the artist. Let the acrylics dry at least thirty minutes.

STEP ELEVEN: Add glitter to the spiral designs. First, Holman uses glitter glue and follows the edge of each spiral; she does not put glue inside the spiral, but just goes around the outside edge (see photo 9). When the glue is applied, she sprinkles on glitter "by gently tapping the container. This way, you will not produce too much excess glitter."

Note: Holman utilizes more than one spiral in her design. "If there is more than one design element that you wish to glitter, do each one at a time and allow it to dry before moving on to the next."

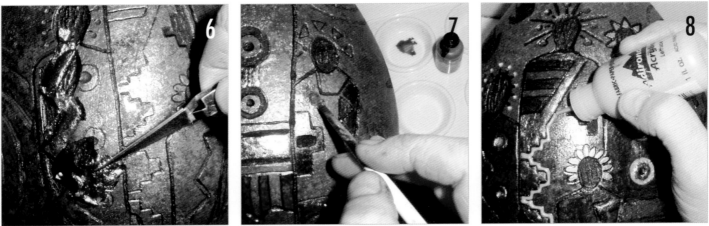

STEP TWELVE: Holman calls this an "optional effect." It involves the use of pigment powders and a glazing medium. Holman puts both substances side by side, then takes a stipple brush and dabs it in the medium, into the powder, and onto the surface of the gourd (see photo 10). "Lightly dab, dab, dab the mixed powder and glaze onto and around the gourd. Use just enough to give the gourd an additional light metallic glazed appearance." Let the powder and glaze mixture dry for at least thirty minutes.

STEP THIRTEEN: Take a good look at the finished product and survey the results! Happy? Good! Protect the piece by spraying on a light coat of polyurethane or other finish.

Tip: Holman says: "If you want to add some pizzazz to your finished gourd, try decorative feathers or bead embellishment on top! Or, place your completed gourd on a decorative stand that helps bring out the unique beauty of your artwork. Be proud of yourself and show off what you created!"

9

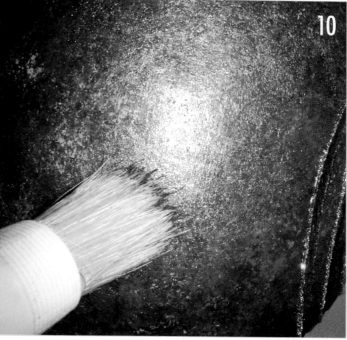

10

Artist

Cindy Lee

You won't actually have this opportunity, but were you to venture into Cindy Lee's Folsom, California, backyard, you wouldn't find all that much to look at unless you share her fascination with gourds. That's the only thing growing back there, really—gourds, and the uninvited dandelion or morning glory. The important thing is that Lee finds an entire world to examine every time she goes out the back door—a world populated by unique shapes just waiting for artistic vision.

"My work is an expression of the uplifting joy I find in nature," Lee says, "one of the reasons I chose to work with gourds." The transition to gourds happened a few years ago while teaching weaving for an environmental living course at her children's school. "The discussion moved from weaving fabric to baskets to the use of gourds by pioneers and Native Americans. After some research and experimentation, I became captivated by the artistic possibilities of hard-shell gourds."

Key to this fascination was Lee's interest in history and culture. Through study, Lee has seen how artists, musicians and spiritual leaders incorporated timeless design and respect for the natural world into their creations; she endeavors to do exactly the same in a thoroughly modern context. "I like to think of my art as a modern continuation of ancient art traditions."

Lee's designs demonstrate a respect for and focus on the natural world and ancient cultures. Her portfolio includes an eclectic collection of nature themes and ethnic designs, including African shekeries and bushel bowls; Asian-themed pieces utilizing calligraphy, washi art and faux raku; Polynesian and pre-Columbian designs; and bead-encrusted bowls inspired by the Huichol American Indians.

Remarkably, Lee does not limit herself to gourds for purely artistic or aesthetic purposes; many of her creations are also functional. Take, for example, the Mbira and Dulcimer folk instruments she creates, or the lamps, pitchers and jewelry she crafts. Each has a far greater purpose than looking pretty, though they accomplish that as well.

PEPPERBERRY

FOREST TREASURE

EVENING STAR

87

Project

PINE-NEEDLE COILING ON A FINISHED GOURD

In addition to pyrography and carving, one of Lee's most frequently used decorative techniques is pine-needle coiling. In this process, Lee uses either gathered or purchased pine needles to create a decorative edge, reminiscent of weaving, on a gourd. In keeping with her practice, the gourds with pine-needle coiling are based on Native American basketry. The pine needles can be used to expand the volume of the finished piece, frame or decorate the rim, or create a very distinctive decorative lid.

MATERIALS
- Acrylic paint: cream-chocolate brown
- Artificial sinew: natural color
- Gourd
- Leather dye: cardovan
- Pendant or large bead
- Pine needles: approximately 5 oz.
- Polyurethane
- Shellac (optional)
- Tung oil
- Vinegar: ⅓ cup
- Wood stain: cherry wood

TOOLS
- Baking sheet
- Bleach and water
- Drill with ¹⁄₁₆" bit
- Dull knife (optional)
- Fabric softener
- Gauge (plastic/metal tubing—Lee uses ½" nylon spacer)
- Needle-nosed pliers for pulling needle through coils
- Pencil
- Scissors
- Paintbrush
- Tape measure
- Tapestry needle: #22

STEP ONE: Clean the outside of the gourd (see page 9). Lee chooses a rounded gourd and removes approximately a quarter on top to create a recognizable bowl shape (see photo 1). Clean out the inside of the gourd and let it dry completely (see page 11). Lee finishes the initial preparations by applying a cherry wood stain to the outside and sealing it with polyurethane. She then paints the interior of the gourd with a mixture of acrylic paint and tung oil in a 10:1 ratio. The paint can be anything from cream to chocolate brown that creates a clean natural look.

STEP TWO: Prepare the pine needles. Whether they are purchased or picked up in the backyard, Lee prepares them the same way: Spread them on a baking sheet and swish them in a solution of hot water and bleach (1:10) for approximately ten minutes. "This will take care of any mold, mildew, or forest bugaboos that are in the needles," Lee says. Rinse the needles completely, then do a final rinse in warm water and fabric softener to make the needles more pliable. Remove the caps (fascicles) when the needles are wet, using fingernails or a dull knife. Spread the wet needles on newspaper and allow them to dry. Gather them with the blunt ends together and tie them in bundles to keep them straight and ready for use.

STEP THREE: Drill holes in the gourd for binding the pine needles. Using a tape measure, measure down ¼" from the rim of the gourd and mark it with a pencil. Then measure around the rim of the gourd and mark every ½", taking care to stay ¼" from the rim (see photos 1 and 2). Drill holes through the gourd using a ¹⁄₁₆" drill bit.

Note: Lee says not to worry too much about the holes being exactly ½" apart. "If your gourd does not divide into perfect ½" intervals, simply make your final marks a little closer or farther apart."

STEP FOUR: Start the pine needle coil around the rim of the gourd. Thread the tapestry needle with approximately a yard of artificial sinew and begin with a bundle of nine to twelve pine needles. With the blunt, decapped ends together, hold the pine needles against the rim of the gourd with your least-adept hand (see photo 2). Push the needle through the first hole from the inside of the gourd, leaving approximately a 2" tail inside. Keep stitching over the rim to the right, securing both the pine needles and the tail of the sinew (see photo 3). "Pull tightly," Lee advises. "Snug stitches ensure a nice, firm basket."

Tip: "There are no set rules for coil or stitch directions," Lee says. "In this lesson, I relate the way I like to coil: counterclockwise, inserting the needle from the back (inside) to the front (outside). If you'd like to try clockwise, or front-to-back, stitches, see how that feels and work the way that's most comfortable for you."

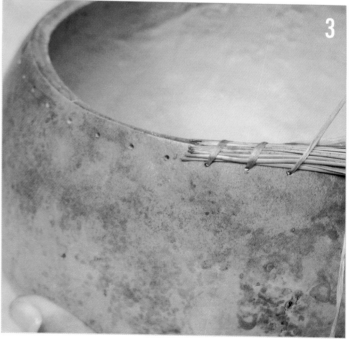

STEP FIVE: Keep on stitching! After the first few stitches, place the gauge over the end of the pine needle bundle (see photo 4). "Hang in there," Lee advises. "It gets easier!" At this point, add two or three needles to the gauge with every stitch until the coil gradually thickens and the gauge is full (see photo 5); remember to add pine needles every few stitches until finished. "Make sure your gauge stays full but not tightly packed and your coils will be uniform," Lee says.

STEP SIX: Add additional layers of pine needles. Once a coil is stitched all the way around the rim of the gourd, start stitching coils on top of each other. For this pattern employ a split stitch: From the back, push the needle through the previous coil, making sure to split the sinew and catch approximately one-third of the needles in the lower coil (see photo 6). Make sure the needle splits the sinew as it emerges from the front of the basket. Continue adding coils in this manner.

STEP SEVEN: Add additional sinew. With approximately 2" of sinew remaining, remove the needle, then take the tail of the sinew (pointing outward from the front of the basket) and pull it to the inside between the coils. Thread a new piece of sinew onto the needle and, starting from the inside, push the needle through the last stitch. Again, leave a 2" tail on the sinew, twist or tie the old and new tails together, then hide them in between the coils as the stitching continues.

STEP EIGHT: Shape the desired basket. Lee creates the shape she wants by "gradually stitching each successive coil slightly to the inside of the previous coil for six coils. When adjusting or changing the coil direction, do it at the start of a new row." She creates a neck on the basket, starting with row seven, by stitching row eight right on top of it instead of offset (see photo 7). The final coil is stitched to the outside of the neck; the entire top of the basket is one continuous coil.

STEP NINE: Finish the final row. Taper the pine needles so they will blend into the beginning of this last row. Stop adding needles about 4" from the point where you'd like to end. Approaching that point, end the coil by removing the gauge and cutting the needles at an angle. Keep stitching until the needles are bound and the sinew extends slightly beyond the end of the final row. Anchor the sinew by running it in and out of several coils, then trim the tail.

STEP TEN: Lee prefers to finish her pieces by applying a coat of shellac to the pine needles. "Shellac gives a semigloss finish and helps to preserve the basket. However, it is not really necessary and entirely up to you, the artist."

STEP ELEVEN: Add decorative elements. To create a focal point on this piece, Lee adds a carved Soo Chow jade pendant (see photo 8). Simply secure the pendant with

sinew, tying a knot on the inside of the basket. Says Lee, "This particular project is great for showing off a special bead, pendant, or that unusual single earring you found at a garage sale."

Dyeing Pine Needles

"Occasionally, I use dyed needles in my work. The colored needles pictured here are dyed with cordovan leather dye," Lee says. To dye the needles, place them in an old pot and pour in only enough very hot water to fully cover them (hot water opens the pores of the needles). Let them soak a few minutes. Add leather dye directly to the water and mix until satisfied with the intensity of color. Once the color desired I achieved, rinse the needles with cold water until the water runs clear, then do a final rinse with one quart water to $1/3$ cup vinegar. "The vinegar acts as a mordant, setting the dye. Let the needles dry thoroughly before bundling."

Barbara Lewis

Only a year into her gourd-crafting journey, Barbara Lewis is an ideal example of what one person can achieve artistically when inspired by a particular medium. In February of 2004, armed with basically the first three gourds she had ever created, Lewis entered the Arizona State Gourd Festival to compete against 257 other artists. "I am so new at this, I don't know what to expect." Lewis said at the time. "This is my first attempt at gourd art." But when the proverbial smoke had cleared, all three of her gourds had earned a ribbon. "I won a first, a second, and a third. All my entries won!"

Currently a resident of New Mexico, Lewis became fascinated with gourds after seeing the work of other artists and realizing what a fantastic medium the gourd could be. "I have always favored three-dimensional art forms," she says, "I've done leather creations, bead design and pottery." Gourds, however, held a particular fascination given their natural state as a creative canvas. "I was hooked!"

Another aspect of the craft that appeals to Lewis is the history of gourds and their use in artistic endeavors. But while history records the use of gourds, and pieces have even been found in the burial tombs of various ancient cultures, it is the modern world and its capabilities that make the craft interesting. "The tools, equipment, and color applications available to the artists of today have refined the art of gourd decoration and have made it possible to explore endless creative avenues in pursuit of the elegant and the unusual," Lewis says.

With a degree in fine arts from the University of Wisconsin, Lewis's artistic muse previously led her to watercolors, and she has also enjoyed forays into architecture and design while living in Wisconsin and Colorado.

It is fair to say that Lewis is still happily within the gourd honeymoon period, a state that perhaps lasts indefinitely for true gourd aficionados. "I encourage anyone with a desire to create to explore the world of gourds," she says. "Find out for yourselves how rewarding the adventure can be."

SOUTHWEST AUTUMN

SUN CIRCLE

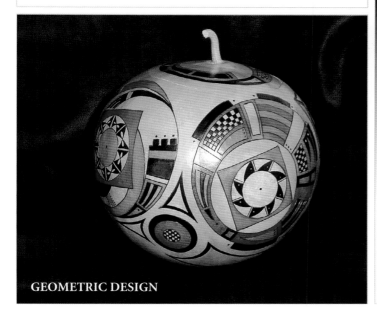

GEOMETRIC DESIGN

GILA MONSTER

Project

GEOMETRIC DESIGNS

Central to the creation of Lewis's gourds is the use of geometric shapes. "Since gourds are rounded," she says, "circular designs flow well and can be enhanced with your choice of design in the center or around circles and squares." Of course, creating geometric designs on a convex surface is different from doing so on a flat surface, and "the following steps," she adds, "should help you create designs that are concise in their configurations."

MATERIALS
- Acrylic paints: assorted colors
- Gourd
- Leather dyes: assorted colors
- Technical pens
- UV protective spray sealer: matte finish

TOOLS
- Compass
- Cotton swabs
- Craft Knife
- Denatured alcohol
- Embroidery hoops: assorted
- Heavy-weight paper for templates
- Mini jigsaw
- Paintbrushes: small
- Pencil
- Soft cloth
- Soft tape measure
- Wet/dry sandpaper: fine grit
- Wood-burning system

STEP ONE: Clean the outside of the gourd (see page 9). Lewis recommends a light-colored gourd with no darkly blemished areas. She also suggests a "very round gourd" to facilitate the use of circular patterns.

STEP TWO: Cut a lid from the top of the gourd. Lewis uses an embroidery hoop to create a perfectly round line to follow (see photo 1). She then cuts open the gourd, using a mini jigsaw. Clean out the inside of the gourd (see pages 11).

STEP THREE: Develop a mental picture of the desired design. It will probably be helpful before actually drawing on the gourd to develop a concept on paper. Determine whether the lid will be part of the entire design or perhaps separate while maintaining the same theme and feel.

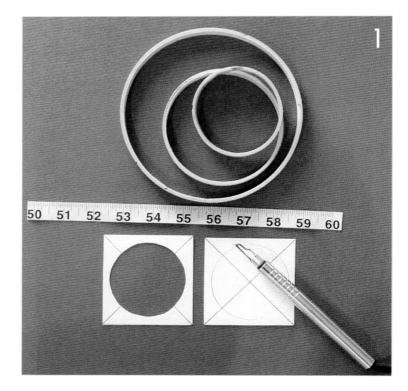

STEP FOUR: Draw the design on the surface of the gourd. For Lewis, this is where the use of embroidery hoops and a compass come into play to create circles. To create squares, cut a square from heavy-weight paper, then draw a circle inside the square using a compass. Cut out that area to create an open circle inside the square (see photo 2). This will allow the square pattern to sit even and flat against the gourd. Besides circles and squares, Lewis creates the remainder of the designs either with the use of a soft tape measure or freehand (see photo 3).

> *Note: Lewis advises the artist to "think about your design as you move around the gourd. When done with the design on the gourd, study it and decide on a design element for the cover (lid, if there is one) that will complement the rest of the gourd."*

STEP FIVE: When satisfied with the design created, burn it into the surface of the gourd. Using a wood-burning tool with a standard tip, start with a low heat setting and hold the gourd in your least-adept hand (see photo 4). Lewis's technique is to pull the wood-burning tool toward her while rotating the gourd away.

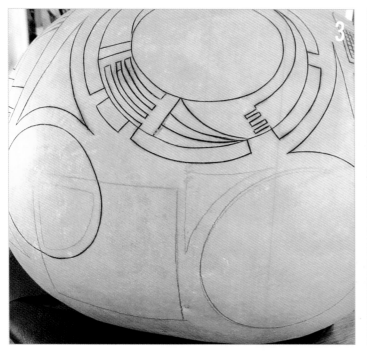

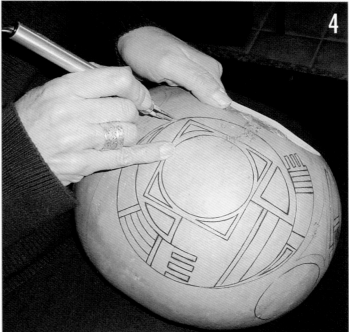

Tip: Consider the thickness of the gourd. Lewis warns that a thin gourd and overly hot tool could result in a hole in the gourd—an irreparable error. Clean the tool whenever burn residue builds up on the tip, "which is often." Lewis uses a leather strap with honing compound to both clean and sharpen the wood-burning pen at the same time.

STEP SIX: To clean up the surface of the gourd after burning, Lewis sands the entire surface with very fine wet/dry sandpaper. Wet sandpaper is less abrasive, and the process will also remove the waxy residue and any lingering pencil marks. Remember to sand lightly the underside of the lid and avoid sanding the cut area. After the surface is smooth all around, wipe the entire gourd with a clean, soft, damp cloth. Now the gourd is ready to receive color (see photo 5).

STEP SEVEN: Apply color to the gourd. According to the established design, begin brushing leather dyes onto respective sections of the gourd (see photo 6). "Since my designs are very detailed," Lewis says, "I use a small brush to fill in each design, letting the dye run down into the burned lines around the designed area." The burned lines effectively keep the dye from flowing outside the intended area. Allow the dyes to dry completely.

Tip: Applying additional dye to already wet areas will create uneven patterns, but going over them with a cotton swab will smooth things out. Clean brushes with denatured alcohol, which can also be applied to cotton swabs to remove dye that wanders outside design areas.

STEP EIGHT: Add detailed color and design elements. Lewis prefers to go back and add small details—"tiny dots, etc."—using acrylic paints. "These small details tend to create more interest in the design and add delicate focal points to each individual design area." She also uses technical pens (permanent and waterproof) for very intricate designs and patterns (see photo 7). Let the gourd dry completely before moving on.

STEP NINE: Add a finishing coat. Lewis applies a UV matte spray to create a protective finish without creating glare. Let the finish dry completely before touching (see finished piece on page 93).

Tip: Either invert the open gourd over some kind of stand or hang it from the inside to apply the protective spray evenly.

GEOMETRIC DESIGN

97

Artist

Melynda Lotven

At the time, Melynda Lotven couldn't have known she was neglecting her new passion. After all, when someone left four gourds on the doorstep of her new home as a welcome gift, she wasn't even really sure what they were. "I really had not seen or paid attention to them," she recalls now. "I left them alone on my doorstep while moving and settling my family into our new home."

In time, the gourds gathered mold and started to appear a tad unsightly. "One day I thought maybe it was time to get rid of these eyesores," Lotven says. "I picked one up and to my surprise it was hard, light, and it rattled." After scrubbing off the unappealing growth and asking a few questions of neighbors, she learned that these hollow, rattling objects could actually be the subject of artistic endeavor. As a watercolor artist with finished pieces for sale in nearby Columbia, Missouri, she was definitely intrigued.

By the following year, Lotven had identified local gourd growers and was entering her first show, the 1992 Hartsburg Pumpkin Festival. "They were a hit and I did quite well," she recalls. "I now knew what I wanted to be when I grew up." She joined the local chapter of the American Gourd Society, and has since focused her life on family and gourds.

Or perhaps a combination of the two. In December of each year, Lotven hosts in her home a Holidays in the Country Craft Show. "Twenty or more other crafters decorate my house in a holiday fashion," she explains. "I fill my house with gourd crafts and my gourds walk out the door with happy people." Likewise, more people in Missouri must also be happy to know about gourds, thanks to Lotven, who founded and was the first president of the Show Me Gourd Society.

Indeed, the path from letting gourds mold on her porch to embracing them as her canvas has been both interesting and rewarding. Lotven has been mentioned for her work in *Southern Living* magazine, featured in the *Country Woman* 2000 Christmas Special, and invited to hang her gourd ornaments on the Christmas tree in the Missouri governor's mansion.

SANTA TRIO

DOGS

SCULPTED OLD LADY

SANTAS WITH BEARDS

Project

THE CHEF

In painting gourds, Lotven's forte is absolutely color and expression. Like animated motion picture characters, she is able to create complex personalities in facial features, clothing, tufts of hair, and implied action. One almost expects a particular piece to speak. "The gourd knows what it is and I just listen," Lotven explains. "This gourd definitely said 'I am a chef.'"

MATERIALS
• Acrylic paints: black, blue, nutmeg brown, flesh tone, gray, red, tan, white
• Gourd
• Varnish: water-based brush-on

TOOLS
• Flexible ruler
• Paintbrushes (5 total): ¼", ½", and 1" flats, detail, small round
• Pencil

STEP ONE: Clean the outside of the gourd (see page 9). Make certain it is completely dry and cured. For The Chef, Lotven chooses a gourd that is about 8" tall and 5" wide at the base.

STEP TWO: Apply a base coat to the gourd, using either the 1" or ½" flat brush. Paint the entire gourd with white acrylic and allow it to dry completely. Brush on a second base coat for good coverage (see photo 1). Let dry completely.

STEP THREE: Start adding color and clothing details. Using the ¼" flat brush and a blend of gray and white paints, outline the chef's hat, jacket, and scarf. With the same size brush, apply flesh tones to the face and black hair with flecks of white to indicate a few gray hairs (see photo 2).

Note: Lotven chooses to not use pencils and patterns for most projects. She does, however, use a pencil on the scarf here so it is easier to see where it will be. "With acrylic paint you really can never make a mistake. Just let it dry and go over any mistakes you may have made."

STEP FOUR: Give the chef his bread. Using the small round brush and then the detail brush, Lotven employs tan for the French bread with nutmeg brown details and cream highlights. She also uses black and white to shade the scarf falling down the chef's back, and flesh tone with brown accents to create chubby hands holding the bread (see photo 3).

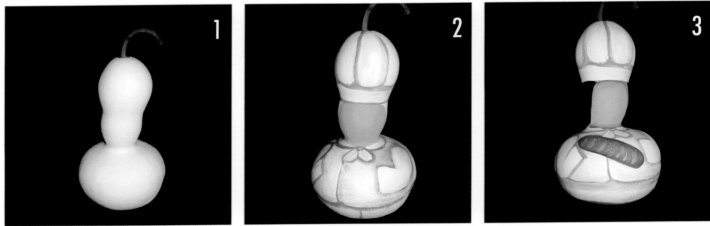

STEP FIVE: Create the chef's face. First, use the ¼" flat brush and apply a white base coat for the eyes. Next, mix flesh tone and brown to shape the nose and create detail and texture around the eyes. Mix a little red with flesh tone to give the chef rosy cheeks and a bottom lip, then black for both his long mustache (slightly curled at the ends) and eyebrows. Add white flecks to the mustache as in the hair. To finish the eyes, Lotven uses the ¼" flat brush to create blue eyes with a narrow black border. When this dries completely, she uses a small detail brush to add a drop of black for the pupil and a speck of white in the corner of the eye as a reflection (see photo 4).

STEP SIX: Paint the base of the gourd gray and let it dry completely before giving the chef two black feet. Using a pencil and flexible ruler, Lotven measures off ½" increments in the area from the bottom of chef's jacket to the bottom of the gourd. She then lightly draws a minimum of three horizontal and vertical lines to create a checkerboard pattern (see photo 5). Using the ½" or ¼" flat brush, depending on the size of the checkers, paint black squares on the checkerboard for chef's apron, as well as a few buttons on the coat.

STEP SEVEN: Finish up the scarf. Apply a red base coat with the ¼" flat brush for the scarf and allow that to dry. Use the detailing brush to add shading and highlighting with black and white to the scarf (see photo 6).

STEP EIGHT: Lotven suggests signing the bottom—It is your work, after all!—and applying two coats of water-based varnish to protect His Chefness!

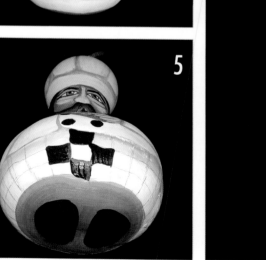

101

Anne McGillivray

There is just no telling from where inspiration will come, particularly when it comes to gourd art. For Anne McGillivray of Bakersfield, California, the muse is common—even banal—repeated patterns in her environment. "From tire tracks in the mud to elaborate embroidery stitches on a crazy quilt, I love to create a strong repeated pattern and then break it unexpectedly," she says. "The eye is forced to stop for a moment and the rhythm continues—the breaks make the pattern more interesting."

Like so many who develop an interest in gourds as a canvas, McGillivray's journey through the artistic landscape included experience with a number of media, including acrylic painting, embroidery scene design, and whole cloth quilting.

Specifically, McGillivray employs subtle change and dramatic boldness in her designs. Where her initial foray in gourd crafting years ago was "simple repeated patterns done with an engraving tool," now she utilizes methods such as carving and glue resist to achieve greater contrast and depth. "The more texture I can add, the happier I am with my design."

But that happiness is not always the result of a thorough plan coming together. While McGillivray aims for boldness and striking texture, this frequently comes about through a free-form process blessed by fate as well as preparation. "I'm a part-to-whole person," she says. "I never begin work on a gourd with the whole project complete in my mind. Pieces seem to work together, as in a puzzle, with the gourd doing a lot of the work."

To explain the approach further, McGillivray does have in mind a predominant design element when she begins work on a gourd and initially focuses on that element. "When the challenge of that section is completed to my satisfaction, the other designs are added to integrate into the piece. With more experimentation and experience, I hope to continually improve the look of my gourds."

DIFFUSION

ORNAMENTAL VESSEL

WINE CARAFE

SMALL GOURD BASKET

103

Project

PATTERN IN BLACK

This particular piece is very interesting both for the bold results the techniques create and for the unusual nature of the techniques themselves. For Pattern in Black, McGillivray employs glue resist to create layers of color and pyrography for a subtle yet eye-catching pattern. The combination appears deceptively difficult to create.

MATERIALS

- Decoupage medium: matte finish
- Gourd
- Leather dyes: 3 progressively darker shades of tan or light brown
- Permanent markers: black, fine-, medium-, and wide-tipped
- Wax shoe polish: neutral

TOOLS

- Flexible ruler
- Foam brushes or cotton dabbers
- Glue gun with glue sticks
- Hair dryer
- Mini jigsaw
- Pencil
- Pointed tool
- Rotary carving tool with small round bur tip
- Sandpaper: medium grit
- Soft cloth
- Wood-burning tool

STEP ONE: Cut the top off a gourd with a mini jigsaw, leaving approximately 1" of neck above the body of the gourd. For this project, McGillivray picks a roundish gourd with a narrow opening. Clean out the gourd and sand the opening and the immediate inside to a smooth finish (see page 11).

STEP TWO: Apply leather dye to entire gourd surface. McGillivray chooses a light tan dye and uses a foam brush or cotton dabber to cover the whole gourd. Let the dye dry completely. To dye the underside of the gourd, it will be necessary to either balance it upside down on the neck or invert it over some kind of stand.

STEP THREE: Divide the gourd vertically into three separate sections. Using a flexible ruler, decide how far down from the lip of the gourd to make a line for the top section (see photos). Using the ruler, go around the gourd and lightly mark dots every inch or so in pencil. In connecting the dots around the gourd, the top section is marked off.

STEP FOUR: Continue the process farther down on the gourd to create the second section, in which the actual Pattern in Black will be created (see photos 3 and 4 on page 106). McGillivray recommends "making the three sections different sizes for a more interesting design." Add vertical lines equidistant apart, running from the lip of the gourd to the first horizontal line. McGillivray makes her lines ½"–¾" apart.

STEP FIVE: Apply glue to the lines on the gourd. Using the glue gun, squeeze slowly to create a thick trail following the top line around the gourd. To create thinner trails, stretch the glue while slowly pulling the trigger on the glue gun. After creating a thick glue trail around the top of the gourd, McGillivray randomly adds dots of glue to the line for added decorative effect (see photo 1). When the top line is finished, add a second glue line farther down the gourd, also adding dots of glue on, above and below the line. Finally, apply glue to vertical lines at the top of the gourd in the same manner. Let the glue dry.

STEP SIX: Add additional colors to the gourd. From the light tan color used in the first application, McGillivray progresses to a medium tan or light brown leather dye and applies it to the entire gourd with a foam brush or cotton dabber. "Be sure to dab well into the glue areas," she advises. "Use two coats if you want more intense coloring." When the dye is completely dry, she applies an even darker shade of brown to the lower half of the gourd and lets that dry completely.

STEP SEVEN: Time to get that glue off! Using a hair dryer and moderate heat, simply warm the glue and pry it off with some sort of pointed tool. Avoid overheating the glue, McGillivray cautions. Just warm it one small section at a time until all is removed and the first layer of dye is exposed.

STEP EIGHT: Look at Diagram A to understand the next step—dividing the middle section into decorative triangles. Looking at the gourd from above as though it were a clock, start by marking on the bottom line with a pencil the points 12, 3, 6 and 9. It will be helpful to use the flexible ruler in making the points equidistant apart. Add four additional points in between the first four at 1.5, 4.5, 7.5, and 10.5. Continue by adding eight additional points on the upper line, one between each of the points on the lower line. Starting at 12, lightly draw lines from a point on the lower line to the next point on the upper line until all points are connected and eight large and eight small triangles are created. Again, look at the diagram for help.

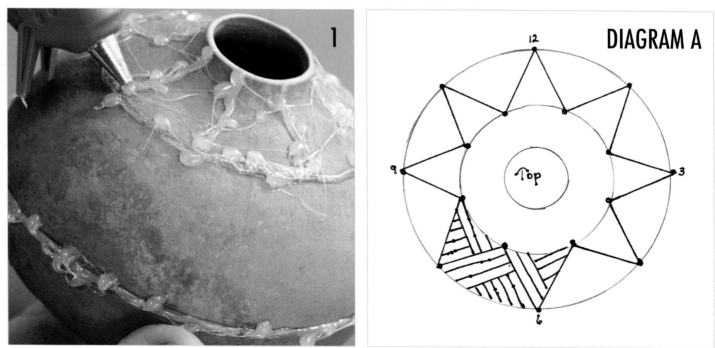

Note: McGillivray says not to worry too much about exact measurements. The patterns created in the upper section are there for creative effect, and don't have to be exactly a certain distance apart.

STEP NINE: Burn patterned lines within the triangles (see photo 2). Using a wood-burning tool on moderate heat, burn some lines perpendicular to one angle of the triangle, then switch directions to fill in the triangle. Continue until all the triangles are filled with pattern. McGillivray makes the lines roughly ¼" apart and tries to keep them "as straight as possible and deep." She also burns dots or indentations randomly along the lines to create more texture and effect (see photo 4).

STEP TEN: Carve lines into the gourd, following the original horizontal glue lines. Using a rotary tool with a small ball bur, carve lines to remove the outer skin and reveal the pale underlayer of the gourd. Carve a fairly straight furrow following the bottom line, but create a more meandering path following the bottom edge of the upper glue line (see photos 3 and 4). Using the fine point of a permanent black marker, draw one irregular line above the upper carved furrow and more-meandering lines both above and below the lower furrow. Draw additional decorative lines dropping down from the bottom line and ornament these with dots (see photos).

STEP ELEVEN: Fill in the patterned section, using a permanent black marker. Be careful to stay beneath the irregularly carved upper furrow and above the thin black marker line above the lower furrow (see photos 3 and 4). When the area is filled, go over it again until it is "a rich, glossy black," McGillivray says. Using the fine-tipped permanent black marker again, add circles and dots to many of the lighter areas on the upper part of the gourd near the neck (see photo 3).

STEP TWELVE: Using a small soft brush, cover the entire gourd with a diluted coat of acrylic matte medium. This will keep the final coat of wax or other chosen finish from causing the ink to run. When the matte has dried completely, add a final protective coating. "My choice was a neutral shoe wax well buffed," McGillivray says.

STEP THIRTEEN: Add final decorative dots. Using the rotary tool and small rounded bur bit, McGillivray concludes the project by sprinkling white carved dots all over the piece (see photos 3 and 4). "Use very light pressure," she says, so as to just take the surface off tiny spots and reveal the lighter shades underneath. "Congratulations! You have completed Pattern in Black!"

PATTERN IN BLACK

Artist

Jan Meng

A close friend once commented that the happiest she ever saw Jan Mohr Meng was the day she received copies of both The *Gourd* and *Birds and Blooms* magazines, took delivery of Amy Goldman's book *The Compleat Squash*, and watched a local garden center make good on a promised delivery of eight yards of topsoil. "Sorta like Christmas, New Year's, a birthday, an anniversary and all-you-can-eat lobster in a 10-hour time span," Meng recalls now.

Such is the life of the self-styled "Gourdhead of Eucha, Oklahoma." Internationally educated, multilingual, with degrees in history and language, Meng seems an unlikely candidate for "near pathological tree-hugger status." Yet there she is, proprietress of the Hunger Holler Art Center in northeastern Oklahoma, where she keeps time with husband and Zen spoonmaster Marc Meng.

Of course, Meng makes her living as an artist, but arguably also as an evangelizer. Active in print and on television, she constantly preaches the gospel of gourds in every aspect of their existence. "Gourds have been used in every phase of cookery and decoration, but also as effective instruments of war," she explains. "Lobbing a gourd filled with pissed, stinging insects into one's enemy forces was a formidable step up from stones and insults."

While Meng's commitment to an environmentally friendly lifestyle (her business cards are the plain brown side of asymmetrically cut cookie and cracker boxes) is obviously one reason for her attraction to gourds, it isn't the entire explanation. A flat canvas, she would argue, lacks vigor and potential. "I prefer the perspective and personality of organic orbs." On a trip through Arizona, Meng swears she heard a gourd calling to her from across a field near Casa Grande. "Its fate is to be a luminaria," she says. "It said so."

With numerous awards to her credit and gourds scattered to the four winds via discriminating buyers, Meng has certainly received validation of her chosen vocation and lifestyle. And what of the pantyhose she used to wear in her former life as a bean counter? They work perfectly now supporting heavier gourds on a trellis. Of course.

OWL GOURD

ELEPHANTS

GIRAFFE

ROOSTER

Project

GIRAFFE GOURD VESSEL

Meng's relationship with her gourds is a two-way street. Most of the time, the gourd presents itself as wanting to be something. "I'll think, 'giraffe,' and a gourd will step forward," she says. "If one doesn't volunteer, I'll conscript one." While this process is effective—the gourd usually reveals itself to complement the project well—the wrong gourd does occasionally slip by. "If this happens, STOP. Start over," Meng advises. "First-rate work demands first-rate gourds."

MATERIALS

- High grade acrylic paints: black, Hookers green, sap green, ochre, pale violet, burnt sienna, burnt umber, burnt sienna, Naples yellow, yellow, white
- Gourd
- Nontoxic protective finish: salad bowl

TOOLS

- Blow dryer
- Large metal spoon
- Obsessive intent
- Paintbrushes: #4, #5, #6 rounds
- Pencil: #2
- Rotary tool with #194 and #9901 carving bits
- Sandpapers: coarse grit, medium grit
- Soft, lint-free cloth
- Wood-burning tool: 30 watt with bullet tip

STEP ONE: Clean the exterior of the gourd (see page 9). For the giraffes, Meng selects a large gourd roughly 24" high and 11" across. Using a #2 pencil, sketch the design you've conceived onto the outside of the gourd (see photo 1). If starting on the gourd itself is not absolutely comfortable, it may be helpful to first draw the sketch on paper.

Note: Meng says that in creating her vessels and bowls, she considers what negative space will look like as well as positive. "What will the carved-out areas look like? What will the edge of the bowl look like?" She also draws strong elements—the giraffes—almost completely, with vague renderings of flora and perhaps other minor fauna.

STEP TWO: Burn the pencil sketch into the gourd. Using a wood-burning tool with the bullet-shaped tip—"The only one I've ever used," Meng says—trace the sketch. Meng likes to use the wood-burning tool in the creation of "subtle color changes," and prefers to create rocks, trees, and other background items entirely with the tool, skipping pencil rendering of these items (see photo 2).

Tip: On items like trees, for example, Meng says she likes to "hold the iron strongly in place to get a real dark burn for texture and shading." While her choice may be the bullet-shaped tip for the wood-burning tool, she advises others to "use what you are comfortable with."

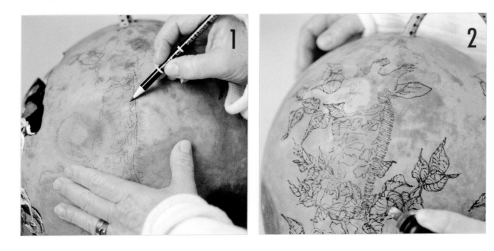

STEP THREE: Carve out parts of the gourd, using a rotary tool. Meng uses bits #194 and #9901, and finds that these "are sufficient for everything I do." Using the #194 bit, carve the gourd, following the burned lines of the giraffe's head, then the foliage, etc. (see photo 3). "Essentially, you carve the top off the gourd," Meng explains. Although she doesn't actually carve the top off Giraffe Gourd Vessel, she frequently does use this technique (see gallery on page 109).

STEP FOUR: Clean out the inside of the gourd (see page 11). Meng uses large metal spoons to scrape out the inside, and recommends sharpening the edge of the spoons by grinding them with a sanding bit on the routing tool. Shake out the contents, then use medium- to coarse-grit sandpaper to clean and smooth the interior of the gourd. Shake out the gourd again.

STEP FIVE: Continue carving the gourd. Meng says exactly how much to carve "is a personal choice. Sometimes I do a lot, sometimes a little. I also carve definition in the body of the art: lines in the leaves, grasses, fur." Notice that she also carves out areas around the head of the giraffe and foliage that gives the animal depth and brings it more to life (see photos 3 and 4). Shake out bits of gourd and use a blow dryer to remove interior dust and finer particles.

STEP SIX: Burn the carved edges of the gourd. Use the wood-burning tool to darken—to blacken, really—all the edges where the gourd has been carved away. "In the places I can't reach with the iron, I daub with black paint, using a small paintbrush, Meng says."

STEP SEVEN: Paint the design burned into the gourd. This step is highly subjective and very much the providence of the artist (see photo 4). Meng uses good quality acrylic paints and small round brushes, usually #4, #5, or #6. For this particular piece, her color selection includes Hooker's green, sap green, burnt umber, burnt sienna, Naples yellow, yellow ochre, black, white, and purple. Of course, color choice is always the discretion of the artist.

STEP EIGHT: Paint the inside of the gourd. Although she does not take this step with Giraffe Gourd Vessel, when an open vessel (see gallery) is complete and dry, Meng usually likes to tint the inside of the gourd. She usually chooses heavily watered-down and subdued acrylic colors like burnt sienna, yellow ochre, or pale violet. "I want the natural interior of the gourd to be obvious to the viewer," Meng says. "I do not consider the phrase, 'Why you'd never know it was a gourd!' to be a compliment." Let the paint dry completely.

STEP NINE: Protect the finished piece. Apply a nontoxic protective finish—Meng prefers salad bowl finish (see photo 4). Use a soft, lint-free cloth to wipe off the excess, then let it dry. Wait at least twenty-four hours to apply a second coat, then twenty-four more to apply a third. Preferring to let her gourds "breathe," Meng does not apply the finish to the interior.

Artist

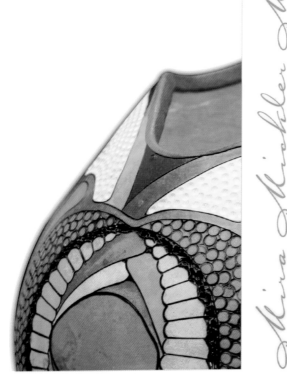

Mira Mickler Moss

How an artist arrives at gourds as a canvas can be as interesting as the work that follows. Years ago, near her Kansas home, Mira Mickler Moss began growing gourds as homes for native birds. The first year, she harvested about 300 bottleneck gourds, many of which "are still providing shelter and a nesting place for birds in our area," she says.

At roughly the same time, the life of Moss's sister Rebekka changed dramatically and not for the better. Diagnosed years prior with Crohn's disease, an autoimmune affliction, Rebekka's health "drastically declined and her disease became erratic during those years. Sometimes the worst happens to the best," Moss philosophizes now.

It was her sister's struggles against a pitiless foe that moved Moss from nature lover to artist. "I was looking for a way to supplement my sister's living and medical expenses," she says. "With the encouragement of my family, I started attending fine-art shows and galleries, which has enabled me to assist her with some of those expenses."

It is Moss's admiration for nature and her understanding of life's vagaries that animate her craft. Gourds appeal to her because they are a unique, wholly natural product seemingly waiting to be enhanced; they are, to Moss, "nature's organic pottery. In fact, some of the obscure shapes inspire ingenious thinking and design."

As a self-taught artist, Moss is directed by an inspiration that manifests in what seems appropriate for each gourd. For some, a nature scene seems best; others call for something else. Arguably, Moss's most vibrant work is found in geometric designs finished in lustrous colors and illuminating textures. While her pieces bear a resemblance to pottery, it's important to remember that the gourd itself first inspired the result. As in nature and life, Moss says, "Each gourd's imperfections individualize their uniqueness."

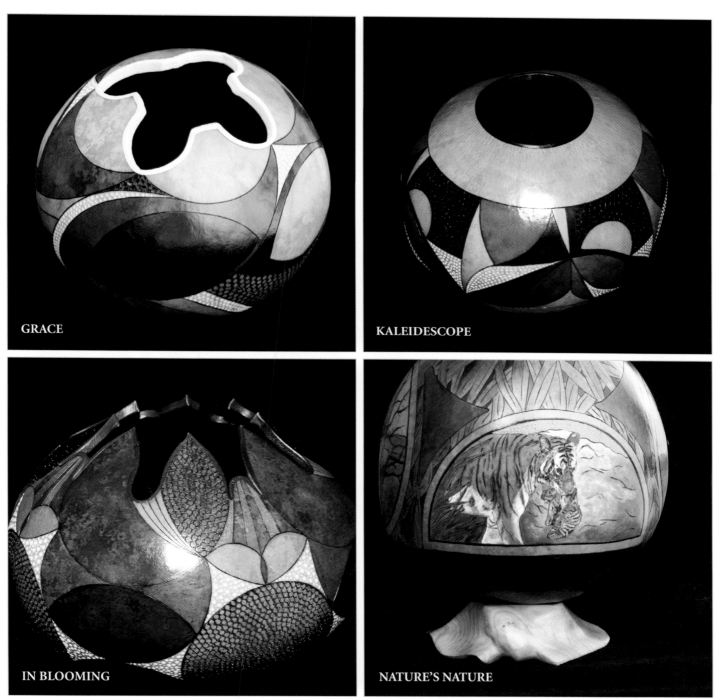

GRACE

KALEIDESCOPE

IN BLOOMING

NATURE'S NATURE

SYMMETRY

Particularly engaging, in Symmetry are the combination of earthy colors and the splashes of texture that separate one segment from another.

MATERIALS
- Alcohol-based leather dyes: assorted colors
- Glue
- Gourd
- Melatonin-based color waxes
- Leather strip
- Opal stones
- Spray paint: flat black
- Spray polyurethane sealer

TOOLS
- Blow dryer (optional)
- Drafting protractors
- Drill or utility knife
- Elastic bands
- Eye Protection
- Face mask
- Flexible rulers
- Latex gloves
- Paintbrushes: fine-tipped
- Masking tape
- Mini jigsaw
- Pencil
- Rotary tool with bits
- Sandpapers: fine grit, medium grit
- Soft, lint-free cloth
- Wood-burning tool with a variety of tips

STEP ONE: Clean the outside of the gourd (see page 9). Moss chooses a gourd with a relatively smooth surface and a hard shell. For Symmetry, she uses a gourd that is almost round in shape and will appear more so when the stem section at the top is cut away.

STEP TWO: Using a pencil, draw the desired design on the surface of the gourd. Not an exact process, this may require time and patience. Moss says that since gourds are never spherical, "the complexity of the design calls for many visual adjustments that give the design an optical illusion that it conforms." To achieve symmetry of design, use drafting protractors and flexible rulers, plus masking tape and elastic bands, to create consistent horizons around a spherical object (see photo 1).

Tip: Though a gourd stand may be necessary to display it, don't shy away from carrying a design through the underside of the gourd.

STEP THREE: Drill a hole or use a utility knife to cut an opening in the area (near the stem) that will be cut away. Use a mini jigsaw to cut out the piece of gourd to be removed. Clean the inside of the gourd (see page 11), then sand the rim smooth, using a router sander and/or sandpaper and elbow grease (see photo 2).

STEP FOUR: Spray the interior of the gourd black. First, lightly sand the interior of the gourd to clean it up, then tape the rim to keep paint from getting on the outside of the gourd. Spray

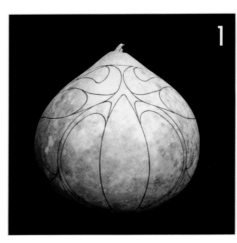

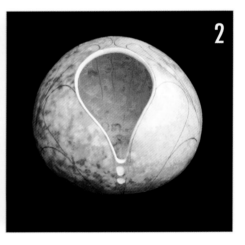

with flat black paint, using short bursts and strokes to keep the spray nozzle moving and avoid drips. Let the paint dry before proceeding. The black interior will call attention to the colorful exterior where a stark white interior would have detracted.

STEP FIVE: Burn the penciled design into the surface of the gourd. Using a wood-burning tool and a fairly moderate tip at first, follow the sketches and make the pattern on the gourd permanent. Add textures to desired sections (see photo 3). Moss uses various tips, depending on the depth, detail, and texture she wants to achieve; she suggests "burning your design in lightly at first, and then going over it again with a stronger heat setting for more depth and shading."

Note: The pyrographed design not only gives you a permanent pattern to work with. It also keeps the colors from running into one another when applied to the gourd surface.

STEP SIX: Are you planning on adding stones as a decorative element? If so, carve out an area where each will go. Moss uses a rotary tool and assorted bits to create two tear-shaped notches near the bottom of the open area (see photo 2). The concave areas for the stones should be the exact shapes of the stones and half as deep.

Tip: Moss recommends using some sort of rubberized surface like cabinet shelf liners to hold the gourd in place while doing tasks like chipping out the space for stones.

STEP SEVEN: Apply colors to surface of the gourd. Moss uses alcohol-based leather dyes so that some idea of the gourd's original color and texture comes through (see photo 4). Dyes are less forgiving than paint, however, and errors are difficult to eliminate after the fact. To avoid costly mistakes, Moss uses "very fine-tipped brushes to apply the dyes in a variety of colors." She also combines dyes to achieve a variety of colors, depths and character. Let the dyes dry thoroughly.

Note: Use alcohol-based leather dyes in a ventilated area; wear latex gloves to apply. Moss sometimes uses a blow dryer to speed up the process on one section before moving to another.

STEP EIGHT: Apply melatonin-based colored waxes. Paint on different hues, then buff the gourd with a soft cloth when dry to give the final product luster and a layer of protection. While the waxes are colored, they won't really change the appearance of the dyes, Moss says, unless a dark color is applied to a light area. Watch out for this.

STEP NINE: Fashion a decorative edge around the rim of the gourd and glue stones into carved notches; in this example, Moss uses opals. She says the rim might consist of "leather, natural stone, weavings, pine needles. Let your imagination be your guide." In Symmetry, Moss uses an indigo blue leather rolled under just slightly and glued to outer and inner edges of the piece (see photo 4).

STEP TEN: Spray on several coats of clear polyurethane to protect the finished piece from the environment. Let each coat dry before applying the next. Wear gloves, a face mask and eye protection in applying the finish. Create some sort of stand to apply the polyurethane, such as either a base and post on which the gourd can be inverted, or some sort of hanging system that attaches to the inside of the piece.

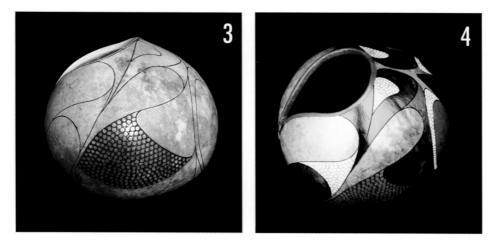

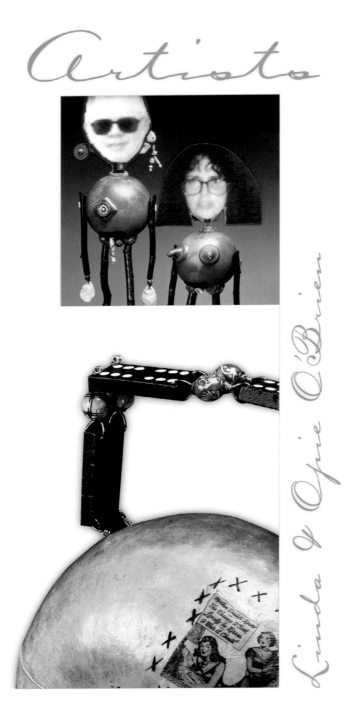

Linda & Opie O'Brien

A quick quiz: What do scrap metal, old doll parts, cardboard cracker boxes and gourds have in common? What's that? No, they're not all part of Michael Jackson's wardrobe. Well, they are, but that's not the answer we're looking for.

To Linda and Opie O'Brien, each item is the source of creative revelation—an artistic epiphany. As mixed-media artists and educators, Linda and Opie define their media as "exclusively organic, recycled, and found materials." But within that definition exists endless possibility, so it says something that these artists would use gourds as canvas.

"[Gourds] are often thought to possess sacred and mystical powers," the O'Briens explain, which are enhanced by fire. In fact, it is the idea of a fiery offering that gives Linda and Opie's studio its name: Burnt Offerings. Pyrography, for example, historically achieved using a burned stick, demonstrates the age-old bond between gourds and fire.

But that connection says nothing about what a gourd can ultimately be. Since discovering them in 1994, Linda and Opie have tried to "push the envelope" on the creative limits of gourd art. Also a musician, Opie creates instruments from gourds, and his work includes an array of percussion instruments. Linda's focus of late is on "wearables," and she has to her credit many functional and fashionable gourd items.

The O'Briens' work has been featured on television and in several magazines, including *Belle Armoire, Somerset Studio, Art Doll Quarterly, Legacy,* and *The Crafts Report.* A guiro instrument, "The Nagual," is on display in the Museum of Pyrography in Australia, and another guiro, "The Visitor," won Showtime TV's Alien Art Contest. Their new book *Metal Craft Discovery Workshop,* came out in the fall of 2005.

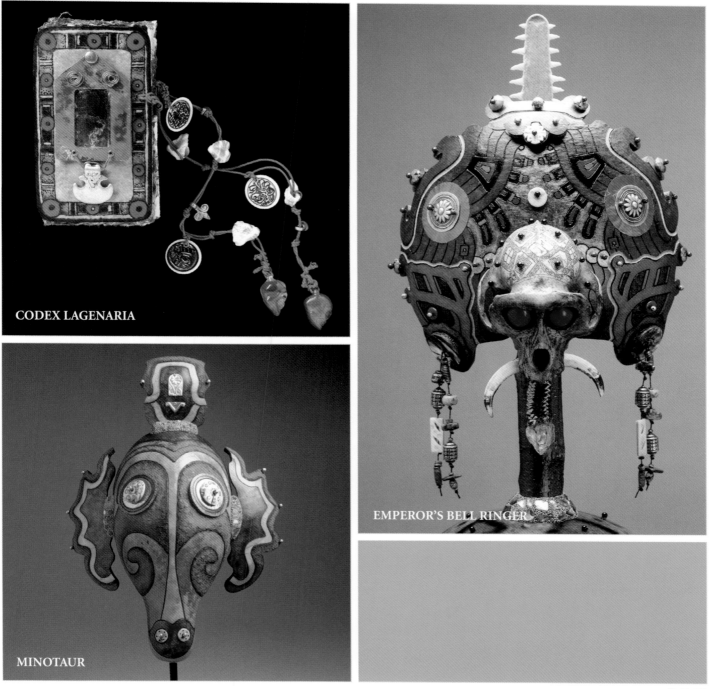

CODEX LAGENARIA

MINOTAUR

EMPEROR'S BELL RINGER

117

CODEX LAGENARIA

Whether they are functional, ritual- istic, or decorative, our work honors both the gourd and the cultures that revered them," Linda and Opie write. Indeed, the Codex Lagenaria project is all of the above. More importantly, it meets all of the criteria established above in the artists' creative raison d'etre, as every basic part of the book comes from a gourd.

MATERIALS
- Charms, beads and/or gourd seeds
- Coloring mediums: acrylic paints, colored pencils and/or stains, encaustic waxes, leather dyes, permanent artist's markers
- Embellishments for covers and pages: charms, collage ephemera, Mexican amate paper, old coin, pieces of leather and 18-gauge copper , postage stamps, rubber stamps and permanent ink pads (embellishments are the discretion of the artist)
- Eyelets: (4) ⅛" with washers for foldout pages
- Gourd, hard shell with nearly flat areas
- Gourd pulp and seeds
- Junk mail: 2–3 sheets
- Polyvinyl acetate (PVA) glue
- Screws, nuts, washers (very small)
- Straightedge
- Thin wire (about 24 gauge)
- Waxed linen thread: red

TOOLS
- Blender
- Drill with very small bit

118

- Mini jigsaw
- Mold and deckle for papermaking
- Needle tool, utility knife, or awl
- Paintbrushes: 1" foam, small detail
- Pencil
- Rag
- Sponge
- Wood-burning tool with fine-tip pen

STEP ONE: Cut out the covers of the Codex Lagenaria. Clean the surface of a gourd large enough to have nearly flat surfaces (see page 9). Linda and Opie use a large, hard-shell Lagenaria gourd. Mark two rectangles roughly 2½" x 3½" with a pencil. Make a cut in the gourd, using a utility knife, awl, or needle tool, then insert the blade of the mini jigsaw and cut out the two rectangular pieces of gourd (see photo 1).

Note: The rectangles that the O'Briens cut out are not sharp edged on the corners; while cutting they decide to round the corners a bit.

STEP TWO: Clean out the inside of the gourd (see page 11). Take out both the pulp and the seeds, but keep them separate: "Seeds will mess up your blender," the O'Briens explain, but make wonderful embellishments.

STEP THREE: Make some gourd paper. (See Making Gourd Paper on pages 120–121.) While desired size and size of the mold and deckle might determine how big the paper created is, Linda and Opie insist a 5" x 7" mold and deckle is easier to work with.

STEP FOUR: Using a straightedge, tear the gourd paper for the inside of the book. From the gourd paper, create one four- or six-fold accordion page, cut to fit the length and width of the gourd covers *Note: From an 8" x 10" piece of paper, a six-fold piece can be created; from a 5" x 7" piece, only a four-fold piece can be created.* Then create smaller books to go inside the larger accordion pages (see photo 2). Cut pieces of paper so that when two together are folded over, they create a small book of four pages the same width but half the length of the larger accordion pages (photo 2 on the left). Also cut another smaller accordion the same width but half the length that pulls out of the larger accordion pages (photo 2 on the right). Finally, cut one piece of paper that, folded over, forms a small book inside the accordion pages on the opposite side of the book (see photo 3).

STEP FIVE: Finish the covers of the book. Sand the book covers on the edges and inside only. Choose a design, then wood-burn, dye, ink, or stain the covers—exactly how is the discretion of the artist. For their book, Linda and Opie choose an Ancient Mexico theme, embellish the covers with designs representative of that theme, then add color in the form of leather dyes (see photo 4). Whatever theme is chosen, sketch the design in pencil first, then burn elements into the gourd, and finish with splashes of color.

STEP SIX: Embellish the gourd covers. Again, in keeping with the Ancient Mexico theme, the O'Briens cut a window in a piece of eighteen-gauge copper, age it with a torch, place a piece of

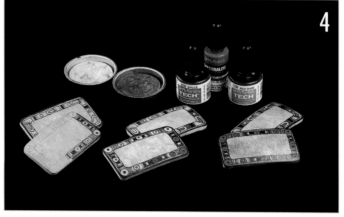

ancient Aztec scrying mirror behind the copper frame and wire it (with a charm) to the gourd using a cold connection method—any method that does not use heat (see photo 5). For the other side, Linda and Opie use tiny nuts, washers and screws to secure an old Mexican coin through four drilled holes.

Tip: "Mica makes a wonderful contemporary scrying mirror," the O'Briens say, " and is available in most craft stores, rubber-stamp stores and online."

STEP SEVEN: Embellish the pages of the Codex. Linda and Opie employ Mexican themed stamps and stickers, and they color some of the pages, particularly those of the smaller books (see photos 2 and 3 on page 119). They use artists' markers for this; oil pastels, wax crayons, or colored pencils will work as well. What the particular embellishments are is a personal choice. When satisfied with the designs, secure the smaller "books" inside the larger accordion pages. Sew the four- and two-page books in with waxed linen thread; secure the smaller accordion book with eyelets.

STEP EIGHT: Glue the book together. Use polyvinyl acetate (PVA) to glue the gourd covers to the two ends of the accordion pages. Slide waxed paper between the pages, bind the entire book with rubber bands, and let it dry overnight.

STEP NINE: Give some color to the outside edges of the entire book. Linda and Opie use encaustic waxes in cadmium orange, cadmium red deep, and jet-black to color the edge of the gourd covers and soften the edges of the paper. For those unfamiliar with these waxes, they suggest inks, paints, or dyes.

STEP TEN: Make a closure for the book. Using the awl or needle tool, make holes in the gourd covers, centered on the outside edges of the book. Use two pieces of red waxed linen, each approximately 2' long (see finished item on page 121). Fold each in half, put one end through the hole, and pull the loose ends through the loop. Tie off each piece of thread, then add beads, charms, even the gourd seeds to each line, and tie knots in between each for a nice finished look. As a final touch, secure each knot with a drop of glue.

Making Gourd Paper

How enthusiastic are Linda and Opie about recycling? They developed this technique to use up much of their junk mail. "Since papermaking is not an exact science, these measurements are 'more or less,'" they explain. "Once you've made a few sheets and are comfortable with the process, you'll pretty much know how much water you should add to achieve a desired page thickness.

"Each 5" x 7" sheet of gourd paper (our preferred size) consists of $1\frac{1}{3}$ sheet of 8" x 10" junk mail, and about $\frac{1}{4}$–$\frac{1}{3}$ cup of shredded gourd pulp mixed with water. If the mold and deckle you use to make paper is for an 8" x 10" sheet, increase the junk mail to between $1\frac{3}{4}$–2 sheets, and the gourd pulp/water mixture to approximately $\frac{1}{2}$ cup."

STEP ONE: Blend the junk mail and gourd pulp. Shred the gourd pulp, rip the junk mail into very small pieces, and place both in a blender dedicated to craft projects. "Add about 1 cup of water," the O'Briens advise, "or just enough to cover the paper, then pulse until it turns a consistency thinner than oatmeal."

Tip: Linda and Opie advise flexibility. "Add more water if need be. If the mixture is too thick, the page will be too thick; if it's too thin, the page will have no stability. Practice makes perfect."

STEP TWO: Pour the paper and pulp mixture into the mold and deckle. With a sponge, press as much water out of the pulp as possible, then turn it over onto a piece of newspaper and let the paper dry. "You can place a sheet of waxed paper and some weight on top of it so the page will dry flat," the O'Briens suggest. "Or, if you're an instant gratification person, you can iron your sheet dry."

Tip: "Papermaking molds and deckles are sold in most craft stores and include easy to follow directions. Once you've perfected the process, you can add all sorts of interesting things like herbs, flowers, etc., to each sheet."

Artist

Dyan Mai Peterson

When Dyan Mai Peterson says, "My life is perfect!" she absolutely means it; and the energy comes through. Even in e-mail, her infectious optimism is obvious. Without exception, she writes "Warm regourds" at the close of each message in recognition of her passion for gourd art. A self-taught artist, Peterson worked in several media before 1994, then discovered gourds, "which changed my life. I'm fascinated with the simple shapes, sizes, textures, and uses."

As they are for so many artists, so to Peterson gourds are an endlessly malleable canvas. "I will always be a beginner," she says. "The learning process for me will never end." In part, the reason it will not cease is that she continues to connect to gourds by growing them; the organic connection from seed to art is maintained.

For inspiration, Peterson turns to nature and a variety of cultures, including Asian, African, South American and Native American. For this and other influences, she has developed a genre and technique called "contemporary figurative sculpture."

Residing in the stunningly beautiful Asheville, North Carolina, area, it is easy to see how Peterson would be inspired by nature near her home. In addition to gourds, Peterson occupies her time raising and training a family of poodles with husband Gary.

An internationally recognized artist and teacher, and the founder of the Western North Carolina Gourd Society, Peterson is also an author in her own right as the primary creator of *The Decorated Gourd*, published in 2002. On several occasions, she has been recognized as the featured artist at gallery shows, and her work has been displayed in over twenty books and even more magazines and newspaper articles.

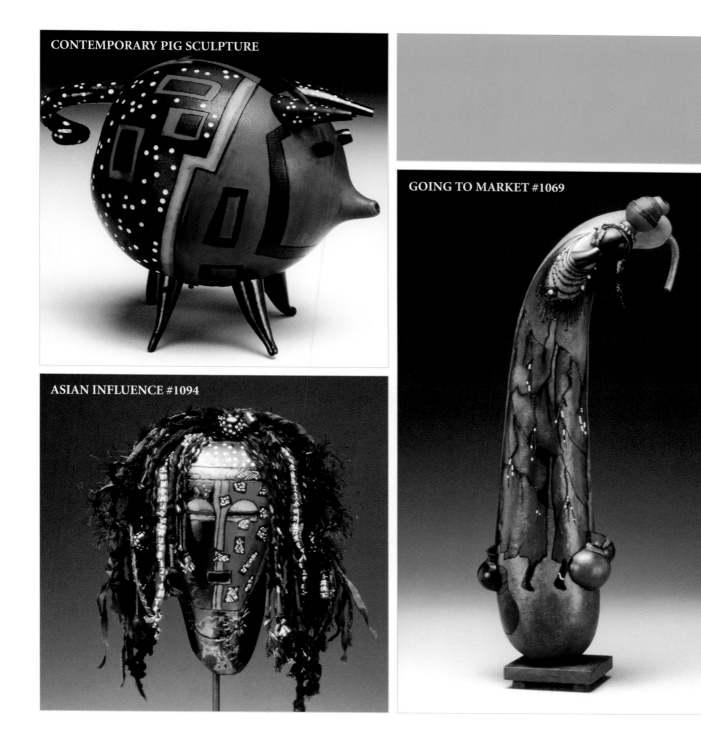

CONTEMPORARY PIG SCULPTURE

ASIAN INFLUENCE #1094

GOING TO MARKET #1069

SIMPLE EVOLUTION

What does this piece call to mind? Exactly what Peterson intends. In Simple Evolution, her goal is to create as accurately as possible a piece that evokes ancient civilizations, archeological digs, found objects. In keeping with a conception of ancient arts, the designs of this piece lack perfect symmetry, and the edges are deliberatley burned and blackened. What emerges is the aged beauty of lost arts and exotic cultures.

MATERIALS
- Artificial sinew: black
- Clear spray lacquer: satin finish
- Enamel spray paint: flat black
- Gold leafing sheets (3)
- Leather dyes: black, light brown, mahogany, British tan
- Metal leafing: variegated green
- Prerusted heavy-gauge steel (available at local craft stores)
- Size (leafing adhesive)
- Stick (tree limb)
- Zucca gourd

TOOLS
- Awl or utility knife
- Cotton swabs
- Drill with ³⁄₃₂" (2.38mm) bit for small holes on metal brace, ³⁄₈" for large hole (depending on size of stick)
- Foam brushes: 1" (3)
- Gourd scraper
- Hair dryer
- Mini jigsaw
- Paintbrush: #4 flat shader
- Pencil
- Rotary tool with flexible shaft, cylinder square cross-cut bur with ³⁄₃₂" (2.38 mm) shank, ¹⁄₁₆" (1.44 mm) cylinder
- Sandpaper: medium grit
- Scissors
- Tapestry needle
- Tin snips
- Wood-burning tool with straight-line burning tip

STEP ONE: Clean the outside of the gourd (see page 9). For Simple Evolution, Peterson selects a Zucca gourd roughly 17" tall and 9" across.

STEP TWO: Cut the top off the gourd. Decide roughly how far down to make the cut, pierce the gourd with an awl or utility knife, and use a mini jigsaw to remove the top part of the gourd. Peterson takes off approximately 4" and says not to worry too much about an exact cut—perfect lines are not required for this piece.

STEP THREE: Finish the inside of the gourd. Scrape the pulp and seeds out of the gourd first, then sand the interior with medium-grit sandpaper. Spray the interior of the gourd with flat black spray paint. Use short bursts to keep the paint from running, and add more than one coat if necessary. Don't bother taping the top of the gourd—overspraying gives the piece more of an antique look (see photos) and the rim will be burned in a later step.

STEP FOUR: Draw a design on the gourd. Using a pencil, draw lines around the top third of the gourd. "There is no wrong way to do this," Peterson says. For Simple Evolution, she draws lines around the gourd that do not meet in front because of the crack that will be created. Making sure the lines are perfectly horizontal is also not important (see photo 1).

STEP FIVE: Burn the pencil lines into the gourd. Using a wood-burning tool with a straight-line burning tip, simply follow the sketched lines around the gourd. "To give the lines the appearance of an old museum piece turn your burning tip on its side when you burn," Peterson advises. "This technique is a lot of fun because you do not have to be precise."

STEP SIX: Create the crack in the gourd and wood-burn the rim. First, roughly sketch where the crack will go with a pencil, then burn the crack into the gourd with a wood-burning tool (see photo 2). "Burn all the way through to the inside of the gourd." Peterson says. She also likes to use the wood-burning tool to burn the rim of the gourd. This gives the piece a weathered, ancient, "dug up" appearance, and it also eliminates any marks that may linger from cutting the gourd.

STEP SEVEN: Apply leather dyes to the gourd. Using a small foam brush and a light brown dye, color the entire bottom portion of the gourd beneath the lines burned into the surface. Dry this area with a hair dryer. Brush black leather dye onto all the areas between the burned lines that will receive gold leafing (see photo 1). Dye the remaining space between the lines a dark mahogany.

STEP EIGHT: Apply gold leafing to the black dyed areas. Peterson does this just a bit at a time. Brush adhesive onto a small area, following the directions on the bottle regarding drying time. Place a piece of gold leafing on the area and use fingers to pull away the leafing that is not glued down. Continue with this method until the black dyed areas are covered, but the burned lines are not. "You can use your fingernail to scratch away more of the gold leafing and give it an antiqued effect," Peterson suggests. "Apply the green variegated leafing in a few places to add more interest to your work."

STEP NINE: Antique the gold leafing. Using a cotton swab, apply British tan leather dye to all the gold-leafed surfaces, taking care to avoid areas where the black dye is showing through the cracks. Brush on a bit of mahogany dye here and there for a more antiqued look.

STEP TEN: Lace up the crack burned into the gourd. First, drill holes through the gourd on both sides of the crack. Placement of the holes is not overly important. Thread the needle with sinew and lace the sinew through holes on both sides of the bottom of the crack, then tie the sinew into a knot on the outside of the gourd. Cut the sinew and continue threading and tying knots all the way up the crack (see photo 2).

STEP ELEVEN: Add decorative elements to the gourd. Peterson carves Asian symbols and similar designs underneath the lowest burned line all the way around the gourd. She adds similar symbols and designs above the top burned line (see photos). Finally, she uses a pencil to draw a square in the mahogany area to the left of the crack, then carves the square into the gourd and fills it with Asian symbols and designs.

STEP TWELVE: Clean up and protect the piece. Look for saw marks at the top of the gourd and burn over them with the wood-burning tool and a moderate pen. "To protect the surface, spray a light mist of clear satin lacquer spray finish over the entire gourd," Peterson suggests. "Dry with a hair dryer. Repeat this method three or four times until you have the surface well protected."

STEP THIRTEEN: Add metal braces to the gourd. Cut two rusted metal strips with tin snips in proportion to the size of the gourd and the stick. Peterson cuts two strips 2" wide, making one 6" long and the other 7" long for an artistic look.

STEP FOURTEEN: Prepare the metal braces to attach to the gourd. Hold a brace up to the gourd on one side and make eight pilot holes, using an awl where the brace will be attached to the gourd (see photo 3). Repeat the process with the second brace on the other side of the gourd, making sure it is centered exactly opposite the first brace. Drill holes in the brace where the pilot holes are located.

STEP FIFTEEN: Hold each of the braces against a side of the gourd and make pencil marks where the holes are. Drill holes through the gourd.

STEP SIXTEEN: Drill holes in the tops of the metal braces. In each brace, drill a hole approximately the circumference of the stick in the center of the brace and down a couple of inches from the top.

Tip: Consider following Peterson's example and making one of the holes lower than the other for artistic purposes.

STEP SEVENTEEN: Attach the braces to the gourd and finish the piece. Using the black artificial sinew, sew a brace onto one side of the gourd, creating an X pattern in each group of four holes (see photo 3). Insert the stick into the hole at the top of the brace, slide the second brace onto the other end of the stick, then attach that brace to the gourd the same way.

SIMPLE EVOLUTION

Artist

Colleen Platt

For eighteen years, Colleen Platt was an artist working on the natural environment. Now she is an artist working with objects from the natural environment.

Trained in art and horticulture in Oakland, California, Platt moved back to the Central Valley after school and became an independent landscape architect. After nearly two decades in landscaping, Platt left in 2001 "to explore new directions and challenges in life and art." One of the earliest challenges she explored as part of her life change was that posed by hard-shelled gourds as a canvas. "Gourds are a great art medium," Platt says. "I enjoy the fusion of art and nature they offer."

If the inspiration to work with gourds comes from nature, what Platt does with them is the product of childhood experience. "A year living in American Samoa and my parents' tapa cloth collection sparked my interest in primitive and ethnic art styles," she explains, which include "Native American, Polynesian and African motifs."

Platt is a member of the California Gourd Society, the American Gourd Society, and the Foothill Gourders of El Dorado County. A winner of ribbons in both the 2003 and 2004 California Gourd Society shows, she contributed to two design panels as part of the Traveling Gourd project, a statewide collaboration of California Gourd Society artists. Her work is displayed at prominent galleries in California's Gold Country.

Platt works and grows gourds in the foothills of Valley Springs, where she shares a home with husband Ron, and rescued canine companions Nick and Sweetie.

SIMPLY LEAVES

BOTANICAL GOURD BOX

LADDERS OF LIFE

129

Project

CHALICE & BLADE PENDANT

The design for this particular piece is inspired by ancient symbols for masculine and feminine. The 'Blade' is the upper, pointed portion of the design and represents aggression and manhood; the 'Chalice' is an inverted blade, the bottom portion of the design, and represents femininity and fertility. Importantly, these two shapes are united by the diamond shapes of which they are a part. The black circles represent the new moon, the eight-pointed stars are the Stars of Venus, and the spirals represent water, power, migration, rotation, and return.

MATERIALS

- Beads: metal, wood, stone, etc.
- Costume jewelry piece or stone for centerpiece
- Embossing powders: verdigris and extra-fine gold
- Gourd piece: at least 6" x 6", good thickness, as flat as possible, cleaned (see pages 9–11)
- Leather dyes: black, medium brown
- Leather lacing: black, 1mm (2 yards)
- Protective sealer or varnish: glossy finish
- Quick-setting glue
- Straight pins: small gold

TOOLS

- Caning awl
- Compass
- Cotton balls
- Embossing pen
- Eraser
- Hand file: fine triangular
- Heat gun

130

- Isopropyl alcohol
- Masking tape
- Mini jigsaw
- Paintbrushes: #0 round, #4 flat shader
- Paper
- Pencil
- Ruler
- Sandpapers: 120 grit, 220 grit, extra-fine grit
- Sketch, transfer, and tracing papers
- Small scissors
- Toothpicks or cotton swabs for touch-ups
- Tracing paper
- Transfer paper
- Waxed paper for catching embossing powder
- Wire cutters
- Wood-burning tools with fine tip, large triangular tip (special technique point or shaping point), needle tip, script tip

Note: More than one wood-burning tool is required; all of these tips are not available for one tool.

STEP ONE: Create the pendant design first on a piece of paper, about 3" wide and 4½" high at the outside points (see Diagram A). Use a compass and ruler as necessary to create a clean design. Adapt the design for the chosen centerpiece—Platt uses a gold diamond-shaped earring. When satisfied with the design, lay tracing paper over it and trace the base design, then trace around the circles and the large diamond (the base and diamond will be cut as two separate pieces). Mark the centers of each circle with a cross.

STEP TWO: Transfer the designs to the gourd piece. Find the flattest area of the gourd and arrange the tracing paper so that the two designs can fit side by side. Tape the paper to the gourd, slide transfer

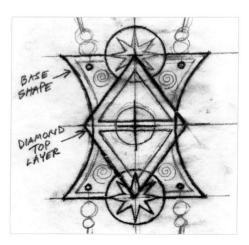

paper underneath, and trace the base design onto the gourd (see photo 2). "Lift the tracing paper occasionally to check your progress," Platt says. "You may need to adjust lines to fit the curve of the gourd." Move the design to a clean part of the gourd and trace the diamond shape, adapted for the chosen centerpiece.

STEP THREE: Cut the two shapes out of the piece of gourd carefully with a mini jigsaw.

STEP FOUR: Clean up both pieces of gourd. Sand and file the edges and angles of both pieces to remove saw marks, etc. Use coarse-grit sandpaper to sand the backs of both pieces smooth. "Lay the diamond on top of the base piece (line the points up with the circle centers) and check the fit of the shapes with each other." Continue with coarse sandpaper to remove as much of the back side of the diamond as necessary to create a "contoured, tight fit with no space between. This takes patience," Platt warns. When comfortable with the fit of the two pieces, sand the back of the base piece and the edges of both pieces, first with fine-grit sandpaper, then with 220 grit.

STEP FIVE: Burn designs into the surface of each piece. First, sketch in pencil these designs: border lines, circles (front and back of the piece), eight-pointed stars, corner holes, and spirals on the base piece; the Chalice and Blade on the diamond piece (see photo 3). Using a wood-burning tool with a fine tip and a heat setting of about 4.5, burn the designs into the gourd. "You want nice, dark lines."

STEP SIX: Add wood-burned details to both pieces. First, burn the four corner holes through, using the hot tool and a needle tip; start with the holes on the front side, then finish from the back. Personalize the piece by burning the date and the creator's initials with the script tip into the back of the base piece. Burn triangular decorative designs into the sides of the base piece, using the wood-burning tool's special technique point or shaping point (see photo 4). Use the same tip to burn the background and sides of the diamond piece, burning darker, deeper, and closer together to create a "dark, textured look" (see photo 5). Using cotton balls and alcohol, clean the pencil lines and burned gourd off both pieces.

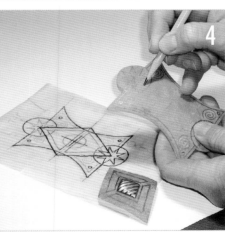

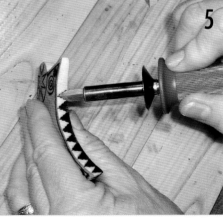

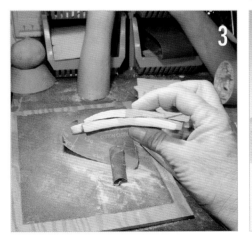

STEP SEVEN: Apply embossing powder to both pieces (see photo 7). On the diamond piece, moisten an area with the embossing pen. Sprinkle verdigris embossing powder to cover the moistened area. Tap and brush off powder from areas where it is not wanted onto waxed paper, then funnel excess powder back into the bottle. Use a heat gun to liquefy and set the powder. Use the exact same technique and apply extra-fine gold embossing powder to the stars on the base piece.

Tip: On the embossing pen, Platt says a dark color is easiest to work with.

STEP EIGHT: Give more color to the base piece. Use brown leather dye and a small brush on the interior section (see photo 8). With black leather dye, make the circles around the stars black, and include the sides and backs of each circle.

STEP NINE: Add decorative elements to the base piece. Using wire cutters, cut the pointed ends off four gold straight pins so that the pins are shorter than the thickness of the base piece. Make small starter holes in the center of each spiral

using a caning awl. Put a small dot of glue on the end of each pin before pushing them into the starter holes, making each one flush with the surface of the gourd. "Press hard with the side of the wire cutters if you need to," Platt advises.

STEP TEN: Unify all the pieces of the pendant. Glue the centerpiece onto the diamond-shaped piece, then glue that onto the base piece, taking care to set the top piece correctly before holding in place for a bit while the glue sets.

STEP ELEVEN: Apply a protective coating. Spray two coats of glossy, clear, non-yellowing varnish or sealer on the pendant, including sides and back. Hold the can about 12" away and spray in short strokes. Let the finish dry between coats.

STEP TWELVE: Finish the piece with black leather lacing and beads, cutting to the length desired and knotting the lacing to hold the beads in place (see photo 9). How the final piece looks specifically is, of course, up to the artist. Platt recommends a spot of glue to hold knots and beads.

CHALICE & BLADE PENDANT

Artist

Kitty Riordan

It's not that Kitty Riordan is anti-technology. Like everyone else, she gets frustrated when her computer acts up, but she still sees the value in technology. It's just that, regardless of positives, movement always creates distance. Riordan feels that society's movement toward the technological creates an equivalent move away from the natural.

"I am increasingly bothered by the emphasis on technology in our society," Riordan says, "and the fact that many people seem more connected to technology than they do to the earth. I feel like something fundamental is being leeched from our lives."

The truth is that modern society is taxing for many people. Riordan's approach to dealing with that strain involves creativity and expression. "Art has long been a way for me to stay connected to myself and the earth," she explains. "Gourds satisfy that desire as no other art form has. I feel connected to something primitive and ancient in the earth."

In particular, Riordan has an affinity for masks. After purchasing two years ago, she realized that just buying the art was not enough; she had to create it. A class in gourd crafts followed, and she was perilously close to smitten. "I often joke that there should be warning labels on gourds," she says: "Caution: Handling gourds can become addictive!"

With a degree in fine arts from the University of New Mexico, Riordan has worked in other media, but finds nothing so satisfying as oddly shaped bitter squash. "I truly feel that gourds have enabled me to thrive as an artist, in wholly new and unexpected ways."

And they've also given her a great deal to do. When not working on gourds, Riordan is tending the gourd patch she planted in the backyard, or planning events for the New Mexico Gourd Society. "I really don't mind," she says. "I have found that gourd people are good people, and like the gourds themselves, a joy to be with."

DESERT SONG

THE ENCOUNTER 1

135

Project

GOURD SPIRIT GUARDIANS

As mentioned, Riordan's real affinity within the gourd world is for masks, which she calls Gourd Spirit Guardians. "I create them to represent Spirit Guides to help us on our journeys, hoping that they may help us find harmony, balance and a connection to the earth." While a connection to the earth may be the general attraction gourd masks hold for the Riordan, the more specific attraction comes from the individual personality each creation develops. "I love the variety and personality. The possibilities of what you can create are virtually endless."

MATERIALS
• Acrylic paints: assorted colors
• Beads: glass, stone, wood, etc.
• Feathers
• Gourd
• Hair material (see Notes on Embellishments on page 138)
• Leather dyes: assorted
• Spray polyurethane sealer
• Waxed linen thread or artificial sinew
• Wood glue

TOOLS
• Awl or utility knife
• Cotton rags, cotton swabs, foam brushes, wool daubers for applying dyes
• Drill with a variety of bits
• Files or rasps: fine, small
• Mini jigsaw

• Paintbrushes: ½" flat, detail, round
• Pencil
• Sandpaper: medium grit
• Scissors
• Small rasps or files
• Tapestry needle: #22
• Wire cutters for trimming feathers
• Wood-burning tool with a variety of tips

Note: In this particular unit, Riordan elects to offer some general instructions on how to create gourd masks. Utilize the skills and principles she outlines to create a truly unique piece as evidence of independent vision.

STEP ONE: Choose a gourd that will mesh with the chosen design, or let a chosen gourd suggest an ideal design. "I always let each mask speak to me as to what and who it becomes," Riordan says. Clean the outside of the gourd (see page 9).

Note: "Bottle gourds are good for faces with necks, and the halves of canteen gourds are good for round faces," Riordan says (see photo 1).

STEP TWO: Cut the chosen gourd in half. If using a bottle gourd, cut it in half lengthwise; cut a canteen gourd in half widthwise. Mark a line in pencil around the gourd as evenly as possible. To make your halves even, Riordan recommends holding the gourd against the chest and looking straight down at it while drawing the line, rotating the gourd around in the process. Puncture a hole in the gourd using an awl or utility knife, then insert the blade of a mini jigsaw and gently cut along the line. Clean the pulp and seeds out of the gourd, and sand the edges with medium grit sandpaper so that the mask will lay or hang as flat as possible.

STEP THREE: Decide what kind of face the mask will have. What will the mouth and eyes look like? What expression will it hold? Draw the mouth and eyes on the mask in pencil, make a hole in each with the awl or utility knife, then cut holes using the mini jigsaw. A power drill with a large bit will also work well for the mouth. "Sand all the edges smooth. Small rasps or files are great for the mouth and eyes."

STEP FOUR: Decide on a design for the mask. This is, of course, absolutely the discretion of the artist. "If you wish to use multiple colors," Riordan says, "it is helpful to burn lines with a pyrography (wood burning) pen" (see photo 2). Wood-burned lines add an extra design element, and keep colors from running together in application.

STEP FIVE: Add color to the gourd. Again, what to use is personal choice: inks, paints, dyes—so much to choose from. Generally, Riordan uses leather dyes. "If applying leather dye with a wool dauber, be careful not to let it run into areas that you do not wanted dyed that color. Cotton swabs are essential for smaller areas and to color an area near a line. I wet a small cotton rag with the dye and rub it over the initial coats to even out marks." For a darker finish, add more than one coat. "Make sure to color the inside edges of the eyes and mouth," Riordan cautions. "After the color has dried, spray with sealer."

Note: Riordan recommends laying out all the embellishments around the gourd before actually attaching anything.

STEP SIX: Decide what kind of material to use as hair. Cut the material twice the length desired for the hair, as it will be folded in half and attached to the gourd where the fold is. Make bundles of hair by gathering material together of approximately the same length. The amount used in each bundle will depend on desired thickness. Set the bundles aside. Riordan says five or six should be adequate "depending on the material and the design."

STEP SEVEN: Make a double row of evenly spaced holes across the top of the mask where the hair will be. The number of pairs of holes depends on the design and how the hair will appear, but there should be one pair of holes for each bunch of hair material. Measure evenly and mark spots for the holes in pencil, then use an awl and create pilot holes. Drill holes through the mask using a ³⁄₃₂" bit.

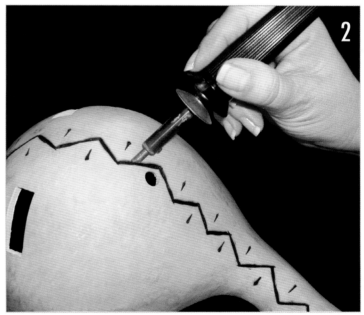

STEP EIGHT: Begin to stitch the hair to the gourd. Thread a tapestry needle with waxed linen thread or artificial sinew, bring the needle up through a hole on either end of the row, and tie a knot in the end of the thread to secure it. Grab a bundle of hair and hold it on the top of the gourd between one pair of holes (see photo 3). Bring the needle across the hair and down through the opposite hole, then proceed to the next set of holes with another bundle of hair. Continue until all the bundles of hair are secured to the gourd. Make two passes through each hole with the needle to secure the hair.

STEP NINE: Decide where the feathers will go, if using them, and mark the location where they will be attached (see photo 4). Use an awl to make pilot holes where each mark for a feather is, then use a drill to make holes.

Note: Riordan says to "drill the hole at the angle at which you want your feather to protrude. You may need to use several different sizes of drill bits to accommodate the different sizes of quills."

STEP TEN: Glue the feathers to the mask by putting the feathers one by one in the drilled holes, securing each with a spot of wood glue on the inside. Hold the feather in place until it is secure. "I leave the mask upside down overnight to let the glue dry," Riordan says. When the wood glue is dry, trim the quills inside the mask so they are flush with the gourd.

Safety glasses are a good idea when trimming the quills, as they tend to fly wildly.

STEP ELEVEN: Add further embellishments, if desired. Riordan says earrings or necklaces might make a nice addition. To add either, simply create the jewelry using beads of any kind and thread, then drill holes in the sides or bottom of the mask and attach the baubles.

STEP TWELVE: Hang the mask on the wall! Let the mask tell you its name! Hanging the mask can be achieved either by putting a nail in the wall and hanging the mask directly from it, or by drilling two more holes and running thread or fishing line to hang it from.

Notes on Embellishments
by Kitty Riordan

- *"I like using organic embellishments, which can include twigs, seeds, pinecones and pine needles, grasses, reeds, wood, pods, shells and porcupine quills. Feathers are a natural with masks. However, if you use feathers, be sure to get them from a store or a reputable dealer. It is illegal to possess feathers from endangered birds. For this reason, don't use 'found' feathers!"*

- *"Consider collecting beads, cloth, leather, yarn, and wire. For hair you can use raffia, horsehair, or sisal rope, which can be dyed."*

- *"You can wood-burn any type of elaborate design or markings that you wish. In addition, rubber stamps are another way of adding designs to the surface."*

- *"You do not have to use a gourd without blemishes. In fact, you can incorporate a blemish into a design on the mask."*

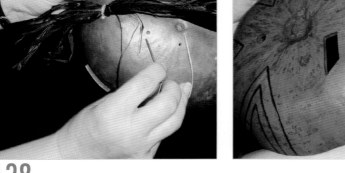

CIMARRON

Afterword

When I began this project, my knowledge of gourds was limited, if not quite nonexistent. I'd seen some maracas down in Tijuana that I think were made of gourds, but not much more. Then I started my research.

Perhaps like you, I could not recognize a gourd in the finished pieces I came across. This was art, not craft, I thought, and was quite obviously created by individuals of singular vision, finely crafted sensibility and remarkable insight. My initial ignorance, tinged with just a hint of ambivalence, was replaced with abiding respect and understanding.

Many of the artists whose work you see in the pages of this book have been working with gourds for years. Others are fairly new to the genre; yet they display amazing skill in their body of work. As a group, the gourd creations within these pages compare favorably with some of the finest pottery and woodcarving, to name only two art forms.

A genuine community of individuals dedicated to an organic art form populates the world of gourds. But if love for gourds is the most common emotion amongst the faithful, a close second, perhaps a kissing cousin, has to be enthusiasm. I have been privileged to gain insight into this art form and the amazing energy of the people who engage in it.

So this is a thank-you—a love note, if you will—to all the gourd artists who contributed to this book. Each artist was unfailingly cooperative and polite, and many put in countless hours preparing a finished proposal. Still others jumped at a moment's notice when asked for additional text, better photos, detailed explanation. I appreciate how easy they made my job, and how eager they were to promote their craft.

To the prospective gourd artist who reads this book and says, "I can do that!" Well, of course you can. Just like your mother said, you can do anything you put your mind to. But having become familiar with the amount of work and the spirit that the artists put into each piece, I would ask that you limit these projects to personal use. These artists have invested time and energy in developing individual vision; were anyone to copy their designs, they would be stealing, plain and simple. In academia and publishing, it is called plagiarism. In entertainment, it is referred to as stealing intellectual property. While more difficult to define, copying art is theft nonetheless, and demonstrates a serious lack of creative ability.

So use what you see herein to stimulate and animate your own vision. Each piece is the product of one person looking at a simple squash and seeing something greater. Michelangelo looked a block of marble and saw the David. Da Vinci looked at a blank canvas and saw the Mona Lisa. Chuck Barris looked at television and saw "The Gong Show." What will your creative vision be?

David Macfarlane

Artists

JENNIFER AVERY
www.excalibursolutions.com/thegourdhouse/birdhouses.asp

LATANA BERNIER
Latanagourds@aol.com

ROSALIND BONSETT
www.pyrogourd.com

CARLA BRATT
www.laughingfishstudios.com

KAREN BROWN
curiousoutlook.tripod.com; kahb69@chartermi.net

BARBARA CARPENTER
www.gourdgeousarts.com

JENNI CHRISTENSEN
www.jennichristensen.com

LISA CONNER
home.earthlink.net/~wiccer; wiccergirl@yahoo.com

EMILY DILLARD
Zvilledill@aol.com

DEBORAH EASLEY
www.gourdartgalleries.com

BONNIE GIBSON
www.arizonagourds.com
5930 N. Camino Arizpe, Tucson, AZ 85718-4612

GERI GITTINGS
www.artbygeri.com
artbygeri@hotmail.com
1804 Palmcroft Way NW, Phoenix, AZ 85007
(602) 254-0919

GOURD ARTIST'S GUILD
www.thegourdquilt.com

LYNETTE DAWSON
dawson@klondyke.net www.picturetrail.com/lynette

MARGARET (MUG) SCHROEDER
schroede@klondyke.net; www.picturetrail.com/muggy

BARBARA HOLMAN
windspiritdesignaz.tripod.com

CINDY LEE
home.comcast.net/~ezmaclee

BARBARA LEWIS
www.studiogourdart.com

MELYNDA LOTVEN
www.justgourds.com; justgourds@justgourds.com

ANNE MCGILLIVRAY
anne1712@yahoo.com

JAN MOHR MENG
www.hungryholler.com; hungry3@hotmail.com;
Hungry Holler, 1589 State Hwy. 20, Eucha, OK 74342
(918) 253-4554

MIRA MICKLER MOSS
www.prairiegourds.com

LINDA & OPIE O'BRIEN – BURNT OFFERINGS STUDIO;
www.burntofferings.com; gourdart@burntofferings.com

DYAN MAI PETERSON
thedecoratedgourd.com

COLLEEN PLATT
www.calaverasarts.org/colleen_platt.htm;
www.calgourd.com/Gallery_Archive/Colleen_Platt_gallery/
Colleen_Platt.htm

KITTY RIORDAN
www.kittyriordan.com

Resources

THE GOURD ARTIST'S GUILD:
www.jkstacydesigns.com/GourdArtistsGuild.html

THE AMERICAN GOURD SOCIETY:
www.americangourdsociety.org

GARDENWEB'S GOURD FORUM:
http://forums.gardenweb.com/forums/gourds

WELBURN GOURD:
http://shop.welburngourds.com

THE CANING SHOP:
http://www.caning.com

FOOTHILLS FARM GOURD GROWERS:
http://www.foothillsfarm.com

WUERTZ FARM GOURDS:
www.wuertzfarm.com

TURTLE FEATHERS GOURD SUPPLIES:
http://www.turtlefeathers.com

BLESSING FARMS:
Red Lion, PA (717) 244-2615

Metric Charts

INCHES TO MILLIMETERS AND CENTIMETERS							
INCHES	MM	CM	INCHES	CM	INCHES	CM
⅛	3	0.3	9	22.9	30	76.2
¼	6	0.6	10	25.4	31	78.7
½	13	1.3	12	30.5	33	83.8
⅝	16	1.6	13	33.0	34	86.4
¾	19	1.9	14	35.6	35	88.9
⅞	22	2.2	15	38.1	36	91.4
1	25	2.5	16	40.6	37	94.0
1¼	32	3.2	17	43.2	38	96.5
1½	38	3.8	18	45.7	39	99.1
1¾	44	4.4	19	48.3	40	101.6
2	51	5.1	20	50.8	41	104.1
2½	64	6.4	21	53.3	42	106.7
3	76	7.6	22	55.9	43	109.2
3½	89	8.9	23	58.4	44	111.8
4	102	10.2	24	61.0	45	114.3
4½	114	11.4	25	63.5	46	116.8
5	127	12.7	26	66.0	47	119.4
6	152	15.2	27	68.6	48	121.9
7	178	17.8	28	71.1	49	124.5
8	203	20.3	29	73.7	50	127.0

YARDS TO METERS									
YARDS	METERS	YARDS	METERS	YARDS	METERS	YARDS	METERS	YARDS	METERS
⅛	0.11	2⅛	1.94	4⅛	3.77	6⅛	5.60	8⅛	7.43
⅛	0.11	2⅛	1.94	4⅛	3.77	6⅛	5.60	8⅛	7.43
¼	0.23	2¼	2.06	4¼	3.89	6¼	5.72	8¼	7.54
⅜	0.34	2⅜	2.17	4⅜	4.00	6⅜	5.83	8⅜	7.66
⅝	0.46	2½	2.29	4½	4.11	6½	5.94	8½	7.77
⅝	0.57	2⅝	2.40	4⅝	4.23	6⅝	6.06	8⅝	7.89
¾	0.69	2¾	2.51	4¾	4.34	6¾	6.17	8¾	8.00
⅞	0.80	2⅞	2.63	4⅞	4.46	6⅞	6.29	8⅞	8.12
1	0.91	3	2.74	5	4.57	7	6.40	9	8.23
1¼	1.03	3¼	2.86	5⅛	4.69	7¼	6.52	9⅛	8.34
1¼	1.14	3¼	2.97	5¼	4.80	7¼	6.63	9¼	8.46
1⅜	1.26	3⅜	3.09	5⅜	4.91	7⅜	6.74	9⅜	8.57
1½	1.37	3½	3.20	5½	5.03	7½	6.86	9½	8.69
1⅝	1.49	3⅝	3.31	5⅝	5.14	7⅝	6.97	9⅝	8.80
1¾	1.60	3¾	3.43	5¾	5.26	7¾	7.09	9¾	8.92
1⅞	1.71	3⅞	3.54	5⅞	5.37	7⅞	7.20	9⅞	9.03
2	1.83	4	3.66	6	5.49	8	7.32	10	9.14

Photography

AVERY
Gallery photos – Finished Birdhouse by Jennifer Avery
Remaining photos by Ron Weise

BERNIER
Gallery photos – by ProVision Photography
How-to photos – 5–8 by ProVision Photography
Remaining photos by L. Bernier

BRATT
Gallery photos – Believe and Dream Dolly by Cody Bratt; remaining photos by Chapelle, Ltd.
How-to photos – by Cody Bratt
Artist photo – by Cody Bratt

BONSETT
Gallery photos – by Rosalind Bonsett, except Pescado by Chapelle Ltd.
How-to photos – by Rosalind Bonsett

BROWN
Gallery photos – by Dan Watts
How-to photos – by Karen Brown

CARPENTER
Gallery photos – by Barbara Carpenter
How-to photos – #7 by Suzanne Doran, Healy's Barndoor Photography; remaining photos by Barbara Carpenter
Artist photo – by Suzanne Doran, Healy's Barndoor Photography

CHRISTENSEN
Gallery photos – Red Lilies by David Macfarlane; remaining photos by Chapelle, Ltd.
How-to photos – by David Macfarlane

CONNER
All photos by John Conner

DAWSON
Gallery photos – by Todd Photographic Studio
How-to photos – by Margaret Schroeder

DILLARD
Gallery photos – Gilded Leaves on a Gourd by Chapelle, Ltd.; remaining photos by Robert D. Dillard
How-to photos – by Robert D. Dillard

EASLEY
Gallery photos – by Steve Anchell Photography

GIBSON
All photos by Everett W. Gibson

GITTINGS
All photos by Paul L. Gittings

HOLMAN
Gallery photos – Photo (copyright) 2005 Les Stukenberg
How-to photos – by Barbara Holman
Artist photo – photo (copyright) 2005 Les Stukenberg

LEE
All photos by Cindy Lee

LEWIS
All photos by Judd Bradley Photography

LOTVEN
All photos by Helios Studio, Columbia, MO

MCGILLIVRAY
All photos by Michael Ivey

MENG
All photos by Ron Neal, Neal Studios, Grove, OK

MOSS
All photos copyright Prairie Gourds

O'BRIEN
All photos by Dina Rossi

PETERSON
All photos by Tim Barnwell

PLATT
Gallery photos – by Ed Cline
How-to photos – by Colleen Platt
Artist photo – by Ed Cline

RIORDAN
Gallery photos – by Dennis Welker
Artist photo – by Dennis Welker

143

Index